PENTECOST 1

PENTECOST 1

INTERPRETING THE LESSONS OF THE CHURCH YEAR

GERARD S. SLOYAN

PROCLAMATION 5 SERIES B

PROCLAMATION

FORTRESS PRESS   MINNEAPOLIS

PROCLAMATION 5
Interpreting the Lessons of the Church Year
Series B, Pentecost 1

Scripture quotations, unless otherwise noted, are from the New Revised Standard Version Bible, copyright © 1989 by the Division of Christian Education of the National Council of Churches of Christ in the USA and used by permission.

Cover and interior design: Spangler Design Team

Library of Congress Cataloging-in-Publication Data available

ISBN 0-8006-4190-6

The paper used in this publication meets the minimum requirements of American National Standard for Information Sciences—Permanence of Paper for Printed Library Materials, NASI Z329.48-1984. ∞™

Manufactured in the U.S.A.   AF 1-4190

98   97   96   95   94   1   2   3   4   5   6   7   8   9   10

CONTENTS

Introduction

Histories of the organization of the church year into cycles in East and West tell us that, after the Sunday, Easter was for long the only feast celebrated by Christians. It first emerges in the middle of the second century as "the day that the Lord has made" and seems to have been a celebration of the saving passion culminating in Christ's resurrection from the dead. The weekly cycle had preceded the annual cycle, going from Sabbath to Sabbath in the Jewish lunar calendar and later from one Day of the Sun to the next in the astral (or solar) calendar adopted by the Roman Empire under Constantine in 321. In both cases the resurrection of Christ was observed on the first day of the Jewish and later Graeco-Roman week. With each Sunday a "little Easter," the spring festival of *to pascha tou Kyriou*—the "passage of the Lord" from death to life—had the problem of asserting its ascendancy over all the other Sundays.

The Christian pasch (*pask*) was by no means a Sunday observance everywhere from the start. The churches of the East long observed it on the fourteenth of Nisan, the day of Jewish *Pesaḥ* ("Passover"), whatever day of the week this might be. The West favored Sunday. The struggle between the Quartodecimans ("fourteenthers") and the Christians of the West came to a head in 190 when Bishop Victor of Rome proposed a series of councils from Gaul to Mesopotamia promoting Sunday as the day on which to observe Easter. Some decades previously (ca. 155–56) the aged and much-respected Polycarp, bishop of Smyrna, had come to Rome to make the case before its new bishop Anicetus for the quartodeciman practice of western Asia Minor. The two parted amicably, having come to agreement on many matters but not on this one. Anicetus said he did not think he was justified in departing from the custom of his predecessors, which was to observe the Lord's resurrection every Sunday—for as yet the Roman church did not observe a special Easter festival. In the event, the Latin-speaking North African Victor, speaking for the Roman church, prevailed, although he was rebuked for his authoritarian tactics by Irenaeus of Lyon among others.

By the third century Easter began to be thought of as *the* feast of the Christian year. In the mid-fourth century Cyril, bishop of

Jerusalem, divided this observance of a single day into a *triduum* or three-day observance beginning on Thursday night and ending through Saturday night as dawn came on. He observed Jesus' entry into the city on the previous Sunday and prolonged the observance for a week, an "octave" counting the Sundays at either end. It was not long before the week became a week of weeks from Easter onward, seven of them making forty-nine days and culminating on the "Fiftieth" or "Pentecost Day." St. Luke's description in Acts of the descent of the Spirit on the Jewish Pentecost was, of course, influential here, but perhaps even more so the fact that Jews continued to observe that feast of *Shavuoth* ("Weeks"). It was a later spring grain harvest festival in biblical times but in the fourth Christian century Jews had long been celebrating it as the feast of the promulgation of the Law. As has been noted, its place in the calendar as the inaugural of a Spirit-filled community, the church, was not achieved independently. Pentecost came into existence as the last day of the Easter season, the culmination of Easter's Fifty Days.

This has to be kept in mind by presiders, preachers, and worship committees over the Sundays that follow. There has never been a "Pentecost cycle" in either East or West, even though the Greek church under monastic influence developed a book for the daily offices called the *Paraklitikē*. The volume was governed by the eight sets of tones, one for each week, which made for successive series (plural) of eight weeks between the Sunday after Pentecost and the tenth Sunday before Easter (an Eastern "Lent"). This choir arrangement was never considered the Pentecost season, however, a nonexistent reality in Christian calendars. With the third- and fourth-century developments of Epiphany, then Christmas, and the preparation and follow-up periods of each, the church calendar became bipolar, a spring observance followed by a winter one in the Mediterranean world. In time the Western church year was reckoned as beginning in Advent. It has remained so ever since, with only half the year dedicated to specific aspects of the one mystery of Christ while the other half goes vacant. Various recent Protestant calendars have created a Pentecost season, calling it by a variety of names, to make up the lack.

In the southern hemisphere, needless to say, the Nativity and Manifestation of Christ are summer observances and the north's

Easter-Pentecost is a matter of autumn. This renders the ancient texts from the Graeco-Roman world about winter's darkness and the rebirth of nature in spring entirely ambiguous in those regions.

If there has never been a Pentecost cycle, why the reckoning of the weeks of summer and fall in the northern hemisphere as "Sundays after Pentecost" or "after Trinity," the traditional designation in the Anglican Communion? It is a convenience of calendar speech only, without liturgical significance. The Roman Missal of 1570 continued the medieval practices of designating the remainder of the church year in the former fashion. The churches of the Reformation that were interested in feasts and seasons held to one or the other terminology. The rite of Salisbury (old Roman Sarum) prevailed in the English Church, which had had as its custom counting Sundays from the medieval feast of Trinity Sunday, one week after Pentecost. Thomas à Becket's choice of his ordination as a bishop on that feast (1162) was influential on the importance of Trinity Sunday in England. Rome made it a universal observance only in 1334.

In its calendar reform of 1969 the Catholic Church, in what may have been an ecumenical move—but also to discourage the idea of Pentecost as an initiatory rather than a culminating feast—designated the Sundays between Epiphany and Lent and those after Pentecost Sundays *in anno*, meaning "of the year" without seasonal significance. Since ordinal, not cardinal numbers are used, the popular designation has become "ordinary time." Much ink has been spilled in the interests of pastoral worship to establish that "ordinary" in this context does not mean everyday in the sense of totally nonsignificant or without importance. The discussion is largely time lost. Every Sunday is of importance to the Christian, whether in summer or winter, on a "red-letter day" (a feast day on the old ecclesiastical calendars), or outside the two great cycles.

Ordinary time in the Roman Lectionary goes from the second Sunday, counting forward from the Sunday after Epiphany (or the Feast of the Baptism of the Lord which is the first) to the Sunday before Lent. It is numbered counting backward from the thirty-third Sunday (the thirty-fourth or last is the Feast of Christ the King in several churches) to the lowest ordinal number in that sequence when Easter occurs at its earliest. The number thirty-four was not chosen arbitrarily. It is the maximum number of nonfestal Sundays *in anno,* given the earliest possible Easter. A fixed calendar would obviate this need but the lunar reckoning of Easter makes something like it necessary. The *Lutheran Book of Worship* engaged in calendar reform but retained the traditional Lutheran enumeration of Sundays "after Epiphany" and "after Pentecost." The *Revised Book of Common Prayer* likewise retained the designation "after Trinity." Members of the Catholic Church who use this volume of *Proclamation 5* need to know that the Second Sunday after Pentecost is the Ninth Sunday of the Year in this Mark year, Year B in the three-year lectionary cycle, while users of the Common Lectionary call the Second Sunday after Pentecost "Proper 9," and so thereafter. The inclusion of Pentecost in this volume is influenced by the Lutheran mode of designation, although that feast goes properly with the six Sundays that precede it, not those that follow it. While all the Sundays from Pentecost to the end of the church year are celebrations of the church that was inaugurated with the Spirit's descent, they have never been thought of as making up a "Pentecost season" in the liturgical sense.

Unlike other volumes of *Proclamation 5, Series B,* which use the Common Lectionary of 1983, I have chosen to utilize the lessons proscribed in the Revised Common Lectionary (1992).

The Day of Pentecost

Lutheran	Roman Catholic	Episcopal	Common Lectionary
Ezek. 37:1-14	Acts 2:1-11	Acts 2:1-11 or Isa. 44:1-8	Acts 2:1-21 or Ezek. 37:1-14
Acts 2:1-21	1 Cor. 12:3b-7, 12-13	1 Cor. 12:4-13 or Acts 2:1-11	Rom. 8:22-27 or Acts 2:1-21
John 7:37-39a	John 20:19-23	John 20:19-23 or John 14:8-17	John 15:26-27; 16:4b-15

FIRST LESSON: ACTS 2:1-11

Saint Luke in the *Acts of the Apostles* (a title he did not give to his second book) has already had the company of Jesus' men and women friends, together with his mother and other family members, assemble for common prayer in an upstairs room in Jerusalem. Peter has charged some 120 believers to choose a successor to Judas, which they do by prayer and by lot. With the selection of Matthias the eleven become twelve again, essential to Luke's ecclesiology, as the twelve tribes of Israel are once more fulfilled in type. This is preparatory to the use Luke will make of a Jewish pilgrimage feast (see Exod. 23:16; 34:22; Lev. 23:15-22; Deut. 16:9-12) to convey the work of the Holy Spirit in bringing diaspora Jews and proselytes into one with Jerusalem Jews as they hear "God's deeds of power" (Acts 2:11) described by the apostles. These are the deeds achieved in Jesus Christ. The apostles speak in languages that are not their own and are understood in the languages proper to the devout Jews from the far-flung places listed. It is a marvel and is described as such. The telling is redolent of the Sinai theophany, a fact that will become fully evident later in the second chapter. Luke is not only recounting a traditional story in Acts. He is adding his own interpretation and evaluation of it to make the maximum impact on the hearer.

Pentecost Day was computed in three different ways by Pharisees, Sadducees, and Qumranites but that need not detain us here. Luke says that "on the coming of the day" the miraculous events he records took place. It is not easy to determine who were all together in one place" in 2:1—the 120, the apostles, or the apostles and the others mentioned in 1:14. Artists' renditions have opted for one of the two smaller companies, seldom the larger gathering. The "house where they were sitting" (2:2) seems to confirm their choice. All who spoke were Galileans (v. 7), indicating Luke's identification of the core of the Jesus movement. A sound like the "rush" of a violent wind (v. 2) is a "roaring" (as of the sea) in Luke 21:25. The vocabulary of Acts here includes words like *sounds* and a *voice*, which is one that *echoes*, all found in the LXX description of the Sinai theophany. This would confirm that he has in mind the giving of the Law, commemorated on Weeks or the Fiftieth Day. The sound like that of a wind (*pnoē*) is clearly related to the Spirit (*pneuma*); the noise filling "the entire house" is a replica of a wholly engulfed Sinai. "Tongues as of fire" (v. 3) conveys the twofold impression of human speech and zeal-inspired inflammatory speech at that. These are no ordinary flames, as fire was an important element of the divine communication on Sinai (see Exod. 19:18; Deut. 4:15).

Filled with the Holy Spirit all began to speak in tongues, presumably, other than their own. This is not speaking "in a tongue," the babbling of 1 Cor. 14:2, or "in tongues" of Acts 10:46 and 19:6. It is using speech for its proper purpose, which is intelligibility. The message of God's deeds of power was lost on no Jew from foreign parts. All hear, not the rustic speech of Galilee, but each his "own native language" (v. 8). The gospel must be couched in the hearers' language or it will not be heard. It is as true now as on Pentecost Day. How many attempts to spread the gospel have been fruitless over the centuries because the proclaimers did not bother to master the language and culture in which it might have been heard? Even in congregational or neighborhood life this is true. People "talk past each other," including preachers and hearers, because the Spirit has deserted the speakers who have not been open to this gift of God.

In Acts 2:1-6 the confusion of tongues at Babel is reversed (see Gen. 11:9). There the ancient author wrestled with the problem of why there are so many languages. Nomadic shepherd that he was, he hit upon the arrogance of those who would presume to build a city (v. 4). This may seem naïve to us but the cause alleged is not so far off the mark. How many lives have been forfeited because warring factions would not talk to each other—or talk reasonably—for decades or centuries at a time. Families have been divided in sullen silence. Friends without number have seen their friendship ended over the failure of one or both to communicate. Where the Spirit of God is, people talk and make every effort to be understood. Sometimes it takes a miracle like that of Pentecost.

Drunkenness is alleged by onlookers as the explanation for the miracle, strong spirits and not the Spirit (vv. 13-15). But red wine and brew in excess make for confusion, not comprehension. The Spirit of God, once it is welcomed by the human spirit, brings clarity. At the same time it compounds perplexity and amazement in those not open to the message. Luke makes use of a prophecy from the First Testament to shed light on the mysterious event, as he will throughout his Jerusalem narrative (Acts 1–12). For him this is the beginning of Joel's "last days" when God's Spirit is being poured out in profusion on all flesh. The apocalyptic portents are a thing of the present for Luke. This is a time in which salvation is being offered to anyone who calls on the name of the LORD. In the chain of argument put on Peter's lips, that Lord is David's "my LORD" of Psalm 110:1 (Acts 2:34), namely Jesus as Lord and Messiah. He it is who must be called on if anyone is to be saved. The whole reading (2:1-21) is a careful apologia for faith in Jesus, worked out over time in the Lukan community. Proclaimed from the modern lectern it is a plea for openness to the action of the Spirit if faith in Jesus Christ is not to be a mere churchgoing habit, a formula of familiar words.

The Lukan account of Pentecost has tragically resulted in innumerable divisions among the churches rather than the unity of the church. "Pentecostal' has come to mean a particular type of Christianity instead of being a description of all Christianity. The argument is over what the Spirit should be expected to achieve in ages subsequent to the apostolic age. Some maintain that miraculous healings, "speaking in a tongue," and preaching with fire as the apostles did should characterize every period in the church's life. Others say that these gifts of the Spirit were proper to the apostolic age and died with the apostles. There should be room for both views, on the basis of the church's long tradition. The Bible itself cannot settle the argument. Meanwhile, all parties are wise to heed Paul's advice and "strive for the greater gifts" (1 Cor. 12:31).

ALTERNATIVE FIRST LESSONS: EZEKIEL 37:1-14; ISAIAH 44:1-8

The Lutheran Lectionary (LL) and Common Lectionary (CL) choice of Ezek. 37:1-14 for Pentecost's first reading is a healthy reminder that the defeated and dispirited people Israel was once brought back to its own land (vv. 12, 14) by the breath of God summoned from the four winds (v. 9b). Similarly, the oppressed descendants of enslaved populations in the three Americas take solace from what God can do as they inhabit their present valley of dry bones. The same is true of any populations emotionally or economically dispossessed. For them Pentecost is a day of unlimited hope.

The Isaian alternative offered by the Episcopal Lectionary (EL) (44:1-8) is a christological text looking forward to the Jesus who gives the gift of the Spirit in the Gospel (John 20:22). He is the chosen servant whose descendants through faith have God's Spirit and blessing poured out on them (Isa. 44:3b). The God of Israel is "the first and the last" (v. 6b), a title John of Patmos will accord to Jesus (Rev. 22:13) as well as to God (1:8; 21:6).

SECOND LESSON: 1 CORINTHIANS 12:3b-13

If the first lessons of Pentecost are richly diverse, those appointed to be read in second place are no less so. The Lutheran lectionary proposes Acts 2:1-21, which has just been commented on as CL's choice for the first reading. For CL, *it* has been the first alternative for the second reading. The Roman Lectionary (RL) and EL have 1 Cor. 12:4-7 in common, although RL begins with the necessity of the Spirit if anyone is to say "Jesus is Lord" (3b) and EL continues by listing Paul's varieties of gifts of the Spirit (vv. 8-13). This passage gives a picture of the church globally and in the little. Not everyone can do everything. There are enough tasks and enough glory to go around. The Spirit active in the church and "over the bent world . . . with, ah! bright wings" (Gerard Manley Hopkins) is a spirit of peace, not of division. Only a trained physiologist or anatomist can testify adequately to the harmony of the human body, but a keen observer like Paul can employ it as a figure of the church. What is to be said of the worldwide communion, the national church body, the local congregation that is torn by dissension, usually over power but using fidelity to the gospel as a mask? Is the Spirit free to be at work there or is God's powerful Wind going against the tide?

ALTERNATIVE SECOND LESSON: ROMANS 8:22-27

Romans 8:22-27 remains to be commented on, serving as it does for the CL as first choice. Paul permits himself to think cosmically here ("the whole creation," v. 22) despite the fact that no first-century person could have speculated beyond the tiny galaxy we are familiar with. He does say *pasa hē ktisis*, though, and assigns to it the labor pains of a mother, in a swift departure from his previous figure of a creation "in bondage to decay" (v. 21). That change of metaphors almost without thought marks Paul's writing style. But the coming to consummation of the entire cosmos is not his main concern, much as he believes in it. He has a greater interest in the human anguish that is part of it, the "inward groaning" (v. 23) of believers who await the redemption of their bodies. They already have the first fruits of the Spirit—the image is agricultural now—which means they live in patient hope of a liberation to come (vv. 24-25, 21). As they wait in weakness they are assisted in prayer by the Spirit intercessor with whom God has provided them. God is the searcher of hearts and knows both all human need and the mind of the Spirit that can meet it. This text provides what may be the most practical subject of Pentecost preaching. Great numbers of worshipers, even the well-scrubbed suburbanites with several healthy children, are in pain of various sorts. They need to be reminded that they live by hope, that their expectation of deliverance of one kind or another is not false, that the Spirit of God has not deserted them. The Spirit's descent into their lives is not a matter of one day but is an ever-present reality.

I sat down in a booth in Midtown IV, a restaurant where the management is Greek but neither the food nor most of the waitresses are. A cheerful woman approached to take my order. I noticed a pin on her neat black uniform, an enameled green dove bordered with gold in downward flight. Sure that she was a co-conspirator in the faith of Christians, I said: "Would that bird on your chest be the Holy Ghost?" She seemed mature enough to handle my archaic speech and answered with a grin, "He's my best friend." Since the word for *Spirit* is feminine in Hebrew, neuter in Greek, masculine in Latin, and genderless in English I decided not to charge her with sexist language. I just smiled in appreciation and proceeded to order.

GOSPEL: JOHN 20:19-23

The RL and CL employ John 20:19-23 as the Gospel reading for Pentecost, so it should be dealt with first on a principle of clear majority.

St. John tells the story as if it happened on the evening of the day Jesus rose from the dead, though a strict chronology troubles him no more than it does the other Gospel writers. The doors behind which the disciples huddle out of fear are closed, perhaps locked (*kekleismenōn* contains the word for key). Surely the phrase "of the Jews" should be omitted in public reading except in well-instructed congregations on the restricted meaning of this term in John (are there any such congregations?) "Out of fear" will do to set the tone. Jesus' first words are the familiar Jewish *Shalom aleichem* but his friends know that the peace he gives is not as the world gives it. His "Peace!" is not a routine and thoughtless greeting (see 14:27). He speaks this greeting of peace to set their frightened hearts at rest, even though they have learned from Mary Magdalene that he lives (20:18). The Father's deed in accepting his sacrifice and raising him up has already reconciled sinful humanity to God, including this cowardly band. That "Peace be with you" is the assurance Jesus imparts.

The risen Lord's first move is to show his friends his hands and side in preparation for the disclosure to Thomas a week later (v. 20). His repeated *Pax vobis*, which passed into the liturgy of the West centuries ago, is a preliminary to the gift he means to give. Jesus has been sent by the Father and intends to send others (v. 21b; cf. the near identical 17:18). This is the Johannine missionary command (cf. Matt. 28:18-20). The Johannine Pentecost immediately follows

(vv. 22-23; cf. Acts 2:1-4). John always does it his way! For those who think of the Lukan account in Acts as *the* historical Pentecost and this bestowal of seven weeks previously a symbolic promise (Theodore of Mopsuestia), or a sprinkling (J. A. Bengel), or a pledge of what is to come (John Calvin), G. R. Beasley-Murray has pointed out that John is describing the gift of the Spirit to the whole church as Luke does in Acts, not just to the disciples (see *John*, Word Biblical Commentary 36 [Waco, Tex.: Word Books, 1987], 381).

No wedge of time can be driven between the two accounts. Each tells differently a remembered tradition. The gift of the Spirit to the church makes of it a community where mutual forgiveness is to be found. But there is a condition (v. 23). Just as in Matt. 16:19b and 18:18, the shorter rabbinic formula employed here indicates that the Johannine community was already granting and withholding forgiveness. We can only guess the terms. There had to be, of course, some proof of repentance. God with the Son and Spirit is infinitely forgiving but the Bible always speaks of the necessity of repentance on the part of the sinner. The church, from New Testament times onward, has emulated divinity in this respect because it has been instructed to do so. There has always been some sort of discipline in the matter, however varied over the ages. Jesus forgave sinners freely but never condoned their sin. The church has followed him in this for centuries. Only in the last few centuries, in a departure from tradition, public forgiveness has been granted in some quarters without condition, as if this were more in the Spirit of Christ. It is unbiblical to think so. The Spirit is not a cheap gift, upon receipt of which anything goes. It is a "hard-bought thing." It is to be received gratefully but in a certain state of heart. Jesus has laid down the terms, unspecified as they are in John's Gospel.

It is clear that woe is the lot of the church or any segment of the church where forgiveness is not available. Are there parishes or congregations, judicatories large or small, in which reconciliation in the Spirit has not been offered to errant groups or members? One hopes not. The penalty of excommunication, after all, has always been leveled in the hope that the person will shortly repent and return to full communion. Some who have been offered reconciliation may reject it. That is up to them. But it is important to ask whether they have been approached seven times seven times. To make the offer is to know the meaning of Pentecost, which is a feast of seven sevenses culminating in a fiftieth day.

ALTERNATIVE GOSPELS: JOHN 7:37-39a, 15:26-27; 16:4b-15

The Lutheran Gospel pericope, brief though it is (John 7:37-39a), has one clear message and one exegetical problem. Jesus provides the living water that slakes (*slaks*) the thirst of faith (vv. 37-38a; cf. 4:14), to be given in 20:22. Surely the evangelist here has Jesus fulfill the type of water struck from the rock (Exod. 17:6). The water-drawing rite of Tabernacles (*Sukkoth*) may also be in mind. But is NRSV correct in supplying "out of the *believer's* heart" when the Greek says "his" (*autou*)? The translators may have solved a problem in gender language if the case is that John here echoes Isa. 58:11. But what if he is harkening back to his own verse 4:10? The "his" of John 7 is probably Jesus'; he is the one out of whom rivers of living water flow. (For a full discussion, see Beasley-Murray's *John* above, 114–17, where the "me" of vv. 37b and 38a and not the thirster or the believer of that couplet gives every evidence of being the one out of whose *koilia* [midsection] rivers of living water shall flow).

The CL choices for today's Gospel are two, John 15:26-27 and 16:4b-15. Both have Jesus promising the *Paraklētos* (Advocate, Helper, Counselor, Consoler, Comforter). This Paraclete is the Spirit of truth who comes from the Father and whom Jesus will send. Without Jesus' going there will be no such coming. It is a truth well worth preaching on since believers are prone to regret Jesus' absence more than they rejoice in the Spirit's presence. His return to the Father was the necessary condition of the church's being a Spirit-filled, truth-guided church. The church's only question is, Has it kept its part of the bargain or has it, in Tertullian's phrase, put the dove to flight? (The master of epigram was here writing *Against Praxeas* and in a modalist context, a heresy that denied that the Holy Spirit was a distinct subsistence [as would later be said] in God).

The Holy Trinity
First Sunday after Pentecost

Lutheran	Roman Catholic	Episcopal	Common Lectionary
Deut. 6:4-9	Deut. 4:32-34, 39-40	Exod. 3:1-16	Isa. 6:1-8
Rom. 8:14-17	Rom. 8:14-17	Rom. 8:12-17	Rom. 8:12-17
John 3:1-17	Matt. 28:16-20	John 3:1-16	John 3:1-17

With the Easter-Pentecost cycle completed, we turn to the Sundays that follow. Trinity is the first of these for the churches that retain a link with the medieval church of the West. The observance, perhaps introduced to embrace God in three persons once the mysteries of Christ and the gift of the Spirit have been commemorated, was enjoined as a feast of the universal Roman Church by Pope John XXII in the early fourteenth century. It was never accorded an octave, being itself the octave day of Pentecost.

GOSPEL: MATTHEW 28:16-20; JOHN 3:1-17

The Gospel pericope should be dealt with first because, as usual on Sundays and feast days, it determines the selection of the First Testament reading. The RL is in a clear minority here with its choice of the "missionary command" with which Matthew closes (28:16-20). Undoubtedly the choice was made because in no other Gospel passage do the three divine names occur in that sequence (but see Luke 1:35). This evidently was the baptismal formula of the Matthean church. It will also occur in the *Didachē* 7:1-3, an argument for familiarity with it in the two locales of origin but not necessarily that both texts were composed in the same place. The arguments for the provenance of Matthew favor Palestine or Syria, while those are just as strong for the *Didachē* as coming from Alexandria. Daniel Harrington (*The Gospel of Matthew* [Collegeville, MN: Liturgical Press, 1991], 415–16) gives reasons why the language of Dan. 7:14 may be a biblical prototype of Matt. 28:18b-20 but allows Exodus

19–20, Num. 6:22-27, the general prophetic commission, and 2 Chron. 36:23 as possible biblical influences. He also argues that *panta ta ethnē* (v. 19) here means "all the Gentiles," on the basis of Matt. 24:9, 14; 25:32 and the supposition that the gospel has already been presented to the Jews first (see 10:5-6). He generously cites John P. Meier's rebuttal in (*Catholic Biblical Quarterly* 39 [1977], 94–102 that Israel is an *ethnos* or *goy* and in this phrase is included among the nations.

Of importance for today's observance is the essential trinitarian nature of the life of the baptized. Upon them, as the church fathers liked to say, an exact likeness (*charaktēr*) or seal (*sphragis*) has irrevocably been placed. Trinity Sunday is the feast of all who claim the name Christian in the midst of whom, as the church, the Spirit dwells.

The predominant Gospel pericope, John 3:1-17 (LL, EL, CL), is just as trinitarian without the formula, for in it God is at work through an "only [a beloved?] Son" in the power of the Spirit. Nicodemus who comes by night (v. 2; cf. 19:39) is probably a representative of the crypto-believers of the evangelist's day for whom the latter has little respect (among them, the parents of the blind man, 9:22 and "many, even of the authorities," 12:42-43). John uses Nicodemus as he does so many other characters as a naive foil for the faith statements about Jesus that he puts on Jesus' lips (vv. 14, 17). "Born from above" (3:3) in NRSV replaces the familiar "born again" (still found in TEV and REB). Although the adverb *anōthen* can mean both, the fact that this is its meaning elsewhere in the Gospel, including 3:31, tips the scale in favor of "from above."

Traditionalists need not worry. Titus 3:5 speaks of the *loutrou paliggenesias*, meaning "water of rebirth," which is to say, being "born again." That single word in the Second Testament (*palin* = again) means what John 3:3 *may* mean in the present instance but probably does not mean. "The kingdom of God" occurs only twice in this Gospel, at vv. 3 and 5. John sets up an opposition between "flesh" and "spirit" somewhat like Paul's, although his "flesh" is neutral, meaning human (v. 6) as contrasted with suprahuman or coming from another realm, the realm of Spirit. Is birth from above "of water and Spirit" a reference to baptism? Anti-sacramentalists like

Bultmann and Haenchen think that the phrase "of water and" must have been inserted by an editor who tried to make John's Gospel more acceptable to the churches. J. H. Bernard and I. de la Potterie are among those who hold that the author added it in a second edition of his Gospel in light of baptismal practice, to show how the new life of the Spirit becomes available to believers.

More likely than either is that "water and Spirit" in conjunction had a history in Jewish end-time expectation well before John was written. The Gospel's author could have been influenced by Ezek. 36:25-27, *Pss. Sol.* 18:6, *Test. Jud.* 24:3, or the baptizing groups of the time like Qumran (see the Community Rule 3:6-9, 1QS; cf. 1QH 11:12-14). As the text stands, water alone would be a way of denoting the baptism of John. He is a witness to Jesus in this Gospel but no more than that. The energizing of the symbolic element water by the Spirit of God is what distinguishes the church's baptism traceable to Jesus.

From the start the church has known only baptism in water and the Spirit. Luke in his book of Acts seems to distinguish the two by having the Spirit conferred on believers in Samaria well after they had been baptized (Acts 8:14-17). In fact, this is Luke's way of indicating that everything in the early church had to originate with the Jerusalem apostles, in this case Peter and John. Throughout Acts Luke stresses the Spirit's activity in the church and modern charismatic Christians read him correctly when they observe this. They misread Acts, however, when they find in this text (and in 19:1-7) an indication of the inefficacy of water baptism. The same is true when baptism "in the name of the Lord Jesus" (8:16; 19:5) is taken to be *the* primitive formula: Acts is thought to be an account of earliest church practice. Like Matthew, Luke probably writes late in the first century. If he relies on a Jerusalem source or sources we do not know what they are. He incorporates the baptismal formula that he thinks likely to have been used in early days, probably the one from his own church. The second-century, widespread adoption of the trinitarian formula of Matthew says nothing about either its primitivism or that of Luke. In fact, in its use of "and . . . and" it may witness to a development beyond Paul's more characteristic binitarian usage in which God always acts through the Son, "in the Spirit" being understood (but see 2 Cor. 13:13).

Returning to the Nicodemus passage, we find it all but impossible to tell when the conversation ends and a homily by the evangelist begins, whether in v. 11 or v. 13. The pronoun "I" is no clue since John speaks in the name of Jesus consistently in this Gospel. Important is the claim for an ascended Jesus (v. 13) who is described, for the first time in this Gospel (although 1:51 prepares for it), as the Son of man "who descended from heaven." The reference to the serpent of bronze in v. 14 (cf. Num. 21:9) echoes 1:51 in that both employ John's allusive technique with regard to the Bible. Far more direct are the successive statements of faith in God's action through the Son (vv. 16 and 17). They have sustained many believers over the ages with their unequivocal assurance that the world is God's world, not the antagonistic "world" of elsewhere in this Gospel, and that God has no basic plan of rejection but only of rescue. Through belief in the Son we are capable of being saved from our own worst selves. The only thing God has in store for us is life eternal, not that we perish through our own folly.

FIRST LESSON: DEUTERONOMY 6:4-9; 4:32-34, 39-40; EXODUS 3:1-16; ISAIAH 6:1-8

The first readings chosen to prepare to hear the Gospel are different in each case and so we turn to the Lutheran selection, Deut. 6:4-9. It is the justly famed *Shema* ("Hear" or "Listen"). As a liturgical prayer it continues with Deut. 11:13-21 and Num. 15:37-41, and is inserted into phylacteries, mezuzahs, and lockets. Jesus quotes the first part in Mark 12:29-30, identifying it as the first of all the commandments. The bedrock of Israel's faith is that there is but one God, the LORD alone, and that all one's heart and soul and might (Mark made it "mind and strength," v. 30) were to be devoted to loving this God. The rabbis of a later time had the *Shema* placed in leather cartridges strapped to wrist and forehead (see Deut. 11:18). They put it in cylinders affixed to doorjambs, often for touching as one entered and exited (v. 20). The mezuzah is still to be seen in many a modern Jewish house and apartment dwelling, while any pendant on a Jewish woman that looks faintly cylindrical is likely not to be jewelry but to contain this prayer. The Mishnah (ca. 180 C.E.) mentions the *Shema* at *Berakoth* ("Blessings") 2. It was probably already in use for morning and evening recitation by all Jewish men in Jesus' time. The word "to love (*āhēv*)" God is not common in the Bible but the concept is there expressed in many other ways. The lectionary no doubt chooses the passage on Trinity Sunday to affirm Christian commitment to the unity and uniqueness of God, so often doubted or denied to Christians by Jews and Muslims alike. Both groups tend to be convinced that Christians believe in more than one deity, usually God and Christ. "Trinity" is a shortened form of *tri-unity*, a Latin word made up by Christians in which the prefix describes the three divine names but says nothing of a plurality of gods and certainly not a numerical threeness.

The RL opts for the earlier Deuteronomic passage 4:32-34, 39-40 which speaks of the unheard-of deed of the LORD of heaven and earth ("there is no other," v. 39b) who took "a nation for himself from the midst of another nation" (v. 34).

EL turns to Exod. 3:1-16 where the LORD's self-disclosure to Moses at Horeb is told, giving the proper divine name as *Ehyeh,* "I am." This sounded sufficiently close to YHWH to the Hebrew ear to be a satisfactory explanation for a name found in other religions of the area, notably on the stone discovered in 1868 in Moab across the Sea of Galilee dating from ca. 850 B.C.E. Perhaps its earliest form was Yah, still to be found in some biblical poetry.

Going outside the Mosaic books, CL employs the vision of Isaiah in 6:1-8, possibly because the chant of praise of the seraphs is threefold, "Holy, holy, holy." The LORD asks the prophet, using the majestic plural, "Whom shall I send, and who will go for us?" (v. 8b).

SECOND LESSON: ROMANS 8:12-17

All the lectionaries feature as their second lesson a powerful passage in Paul (Rom. 8:[12] 14-17) that contains the names Spirit, Father, and Christ. The pericope is "in effect an exposition of v. 9 and vv. 18-30 an exposition of vv. 10-11" (James D. G. Dunn, *Romans 1–8*, Word Biblical Commentary 38A [Dallas: Word Books, 1988], 447). The opposition between flesh and Spirit is not to be confused with the difference between body and soul. It is the antinomy of God-directed human behavior and a spirit that refuses to be led by God.

Not all believers are presumed to be living in the Spirit—Paul warns against those who are not—and not all outside are presumed to be in the realm of the flesh. His warning of death involves physical death but he probably also means it to be taken figuratively: ultimate death of the whole person (v. 13). We might have expected "deeds of the flesh" rather than "of the body" in this verse. Paul seldom refers to the body negatively so it may be a stylistic variant to give the word *sarx* a rest. At the same time, much of our sinning through appetite and ambition is done through the body. The Spirit kills all such unhealthy strivings and brings life to God's children. By definition they are Spirit-led (vv. 13-14; see Joseph A. Fitzmyer, S.J., *Romans*, Anchor Bible 33 [New York: Doubleday, 1993], 492–93). Paul had not yet arrived at the vocabulary that would prevail. Otherwise he would have said that the trinity dwelt within believers from the moment of their baptism.

The whole Roman community, Jewish and Gentile, is being addressed here. All have received a spirit of adoption, not of slavery (v. 15). They are sons and daughters of the household to a person and their cry of "Abba! Father!" is Spirit-impelled, a testimony to their condition as children of God in a new sense and inheritors of the divine legacy (vv. 16-17a). Whatever is coming to Christ is coming to them, but there is a condition. As he entered into his glory through suffering, so must they (v. 17b). The slavery image of v. 15 may be a studied ambivalence, connoting life under the law to Roman Jews (see Gal. 4:24; 5:1) and a life of moral license, in the familiar Jewish stereotype, to Roman non-Jews. In any case, Paul needs the image because of his conviction that in Christ one is free. The whole pericope says to modern congregations that if they take seriously the adoptive status that came with their baptism, lives of sin and anxiety ill befit them. Paul's question is Have they the courage to let God be a liberating and protective parent to them? Life in Christ means belief in him as an intimate sibling. "Fly now, pay later" is reversed for the believer to say, "Suffer now. Glory later."

Second Sunday after Pentecost

Lutheran	Roman Catholic	Episcopal	Common Lectionary
Deut. 5:12-15	Deut. 5:12-15	Deut. 5:6-21	1 Sam. 3:1-10 (11-20) or Deut. 5:12-15
2 Cor. 4:5-12	2 Cor. 4:6-11	2 Cor. 4:5-12	2 Cor. 4:5-12
Mark 2:23-28	Mark 2:23—3:6 or Mark 2:23-28	Mark 2:23-28	Mark 2:23—3:6

GOSPEL: MARK 2:23—3:6

We return to Mark's Gospel today, the evangelist of the year, after having heard from him but once since before Lent. This points up a weakness in all the lectionaries. Homilists who preach to their congregations every Sunday are hard pressed to convince them that there is such a thing as a distinctive Markan theology until this Sunday, when they must refresh their minds on what they said of Mark's narrative technique in the Sundays after Epiphany. This is no easy task after so long an interval, although from now on Mark will be read uninterruptedly until late October. Meanwhile, Mark has already introduced the Baptizer as a teacher who has proclaimed a mysterious "one to come" more powerful than himself whom he then baptizes. This Jesus briefly retreats to the desert, there to be tested by Satan. His proclamation of the need to repent is much like John's, with the added injunction to believe the good news. Jesus collects his earliest disciples around him and begins a career of deeds of power: exorcisms, cures of the sick and diseased. When he presumes to forgive the sins of a paralyzed man he is charged with "blasphemy," meaning here preempting divine power (2:7). He calls Levi from his tax-gatherer's post to follow him and is charged by ritual purists with consorting with such types as Levi. A challenge as to why he and his disciples do not fast is countered with the now well known images of a patch on an old cloak and new wine in old wineskins. Everything is somehow different with the advent of this man.

Such is Mark's Jesus: God's man of power whose teaching is much praised by the evangelist but not provided at any great length (chaps. 4 and 13 are exceptions). Instead, more examples of his wonder-working power are provided at those places. The charge against Jesus' disciples of harvesting on the sabbath (see Exod. 31:14; 34:21) is specious but little should be made by homilists of the shock expressed by the Pharisees. The story is told—misattribution to Abiathar and all (1 Sam. 21:2b)—to lead up to the axiom of humanity's superiority to any sabbath obligation. The saying probably had a history in Judaism before Mark, as did the lenient understanding of it in Pharisee circles. Mark's purpose is different. He wishes to declare the Son of man Lord even of the sabbath (v. 28). This probably means that the Markan church already sits lightly to the traditions that have gathered around sabbath observance and is giving its adherence to Jesus as the reason for the unconcern.

The RL and CL continue the reading into the next chapter (3:1-6), which describes the cure of the man with the withered hand. We have an indication here of the polemic the Markan church is engaging in with its Pharisee contemporaries. Whether it knew them at first hand or not, they are the opponents of choice. We cannot be sure if Jesus' exchanges with these teachers whose teaching so resembled his own took this form in his lifetime. Clearest of all, perhaps, is the first climax Mark wishes to reach in the telling of his story: the collusion of the teachers of strict observance with the hangers-on of the house of Herod to bring him down. The latter would have had even more to lose if Jesus' popularity continued, for they wanted to see the royal household restored and not threatened by a rural wonderworker. In Mark's passion narrative both groups will drop out as antagonists of Jesus (see 14:43, 53; 15:1, 10-11).

Whoever chooses to construct a homily on the basis of the Gospel reading should be on guard against taking the opposition of the Pharisees to Jesus as literal truth. It may have been or again it may not. Jesus' superiority to all around him is Mark's point, that and the clue planted early that he would die innocently at plotters' hands. Emphasizing who the enemies of the Gospel were in the church's early ages can be diversionary when it is so clear who they are now: the amassers of wealth, the people of power and privilege, destroyers of innocence in the young, exploiters of the body at the expense of the spirit. These antagonists of Jesus may vary slightly from century to century but they remain perennially the usual suspects.

The Pharisees can be taken as surrogates for the learned. A dedicated zealotry, however, does much more mischief than the learned do, for it is a class that *has* to be right in the face of all the evidence. Such a power class in any age cannot stand the truth that is Jesus, although they may keep mouthing his name as a shibboleth. When such people align themselves with a political force that is out of power ("the Herodians") they conclude that Jesus, in the form of his disciples the church, must be destroyed. It is no coincidence that Archbishop Lefebvre, the late schismatic, was a dedicated monarchist, that the criers of horror over an alliance of church and state will covertly seek all the power of state they can get. The opponents of Jesus and the Gospel are the same in every age, often presenting themselves as its great defenders.

FIRST LESSON: DEUTERONOMY 5:6-21

Because the first reading speaks of the commandment of sabbath observance and its humane interpretation in circles where Jesus is reckoned its Lord, the Lutheran and Roman lectionaries opt for the portion of Deuteronomy that tells what it *does* require.

The EL asks for a reading of the entire decalogue (Deut. 5:6-21). This is identical with Exod. 20:1-17 except for a verbal rearrangement of the command not to covet another's wife or goods and the important provision of a different reason to keep the sabbath holy. In Exodus Israel must keep the sabbath because of the LORD's rest on the seventh day (20:11). Deuteronomy puts in place of it remembrance of Israel's deliverance from slavery in Egypt by God's "mighty hand and outstretched arm" (5:15; cf. Exod. 6:6). This is an echo of Exod. 8:27; 10:7, 24 where sacrificial worship outside Egypt is given as the rationale to explain why the Pharaoh must let the Hebrews go. Sabbath observance in Israel is attested to as far back as the eighth century, although the seven-day week was observed in ancient Mesopotamia. The inability to sacrifice during the Babylonian exile probably contributed to its importance, for it was pursued vigorously by the priest-teachers of postexilic days.

The commandment given to Israel was to honor the LORD by doing nothing on the seventh day. Christians observed the first day from the second century onward that we can document by doing something, namely observing a weekly meal of thanks and praise (*eucharistia/eulogia*). Their taking that normal workday as a day of leisure was impossible in the empire until the fourth century, when it too began to take on the Jewish character of respite from the ordinary. Any number of Catholic reformers have tried to restore awareness of the religious character of the Sunday. The sternness of observance along the lines of the biblical sabbath by the Calvinist tradition and its North American inheritors is likewise well known. For many U.S. adults of a certain age the Sunday was devoted to church attendance up to five and six hours in their youth. The sanctity of "the Lord's day" has been eroded by several factors: physical exhaustion after a work week, a Saturday night devoted to strenuous "relaxation," shopping, sports-watching, home and property improvement. All is meant to re-create the human spirit. Some of it does. But none of it does much to remind busy Christians why they are absorbed in life's race at all. This reflection takes time, a time when nothing else is going on and not just sixty minutes of worship. The Sunday is desperately needed for re-creation. Changing the weekly rhythm from its present frenzied pace to a period broken by the traditional Sunday worship and rest can be a change of entire lives.

ALTERNATIVE FIRST LESSON: 1 SAMUEL 3:1-20

The Hebrew of 1 Sam. 3:19 says, literally, that the LORD "let none of [Samuel's] words fall to the ground." The CL narrative should be read to the end (v. 20) for full effect. The tale is a justification of Samuel's accession to the prophetic office, of course, but it conveys a marvelous sense of the holiness of that office and of a good relation between age and youth. Employ it somehow!

SECOND LESSON: 2 CORINTHIANS 4:5-12

The semi-continuous reading of 2 Corinthians, coauthored by Paul with Timothy (see 1:1), resumes today at 4:5-12 and will go on for the next five Sundays. In this letter the hardships of Paul's ministry are weighing heavily on him. He has had a painful experience in the province of Asia, probably at Ephesus (1:8). The early part of this letter seems to relate it to the reports he has received on the rebellion in Corinth. He has responded to these by a letter (2:2-4) that he may now regret (see 7:8). Paul has changed his travel plans (1:15-16), not stopping off in Corinth on his way to Macedonia so as to avoid "another painful visit" to the seaport capital of Achaia (2:1). We have no information on the intermediate visit, only that he has substituted an anguish-filled letter for a second encounter with "the one whom I have pained" (2:2-4). Paul had missed Titus at Troas (2:13) so he had no news of the reception of his painful letter in Corinth. His mind was set at rest only when, after he got to Macedonia, Titus arrived there and filled him with consolation about the Corinthians' feelings for him (7:6-7). Before and after today's pericope Paul insists that "we do not lose heart" (4:1, 16) over the mission, a sure sign that he has been tempted to do so. He says defensively that his team has not resorted to underhanded ways (v. 2; cf. 2:17a) and refers cryptically to the charge that his message is "veiled" (v. 3). Does he mean obscure in the way he couches it? Or open and direct but unacceptable to those blinded by "the god of this world" (v. 4; see Eph. 2:2)? Or was it that the Achaian and Macedonian crowds expected an itinerant philosopher such as they took him to be, proposing his own thought system, whereas Paul does not tarry on his own person for a moment (4:5)? He goes straight to the "light of the knowledge of the glory of God in the face of Jesus Christ" (v. 6b). Paul understands nonacceptance of his message to be an incomprehension arising out of its very clarity. The thought is an arresting one for our age. Could the Gospel be widely rejected not because its demands are not understood but because they are? Amidst the darkness in which our times seem bent on enfolding themselves, Christ is a blinding light.

Paul is under no illusions about the fragility of the vessels to whom the treasure of the Gospel has been entrusted (v. 7; for the frequent image of humans as pottery fashioned from clay in God's hands, see Isa. 45:9; Jer. 18:6; Job 10:9). Jewels, coins, and other valuables were often stored in earthen jars. The weakness of the Gospel's ministers has often been taken as proof that the message need not be viewed seriously. Paul says quite the opposite, that it is proof of God's extraordinary power (v. 7). His list of setbacks in his ministry and the resiliency that it brings to light, all deriving from the power of God, is a tour de force of rhetoric (vv. 8-10). An existence in the service of the Gospel is a constant near-death experience (v. 11) but its only result is life for the hearer (v. 12). This passage at a certain point has stopped describing Pauline teams of evangelizers. It describes any Christian who takes the Gospel seriously.

Third Sunday after Pentecost

Lutheran	Roman Catholic	Episcopal	Common Lectionary
Gen. 3:9-15	Gen. 3:9-15	Gen. 3:(1-7), 8-21	1 Sam. 8:4-11 (12-15), 16-20 (11:14-15) *or* Gen. 3:8-15
2 Cor. 4:13-18	2 Cor. 4:13—5:1	2 Cor. 4:13-18	2 Cor. 4:13—5:1
Mark 3:20-35	Mark 3:20-35	Mark 3:20-35	Mark 3:20-35

SECOND LESSON: 2 CORINTHIANS 4:13—5:1

In an attempt to maintain the momentum generated by last week's second reading—which homilists who plan to preach on today's might quickly review—we turn to the pericope that follows immediately in 2 Corinthians 4. Last week's reading left off at v. 12, "So death is at work in us, but life in you." Paul resumes the thought in vv. 15 and 16: Grace is extended to more and more people through his ministry. His "inner nature" or spirit finds daily renewal even though his body, his "outer nature" is wasting away. Reflections like these are a commonplace with caregivers, not just ministers of the Gospel. People in the healing professions, counselors, parents, adult children whose parents live with them—all wonder on occasion if there is any end to the giving, the seemingly constant expectation that they will *be there*. Paul reassures himself by saying: "We do not lose heart" (v. 16a). As one who expects shortly to "be with the Lord," he at least has the certitude that his momentary affliction, as he calls it (the painful experience of 1:8?), is a preparation for "an eternal weight of glory beyond all measure" (v. 17).

To read the diaries, the tombstones, and the correspondence of devoted Christians of as recently as the last century is to learn how present the "things unseen" of v. 18 were to them. They thought the present life not only temporary, perhaps because of its brevity, but a screen obscuring the life that lay beyond. That manner of thought marks very few of today's most devoted believers. Improved health care, labor-saving devices, and increased life spans tie us ever tighter to the only existence we know. Some, like the very ill or long-term emotional sufferers, beg for release from this life. If they are believers, Paul's *ta aiōnia* of v. 18, the "life of the final eon" which, like the ancient Greeks, we call eternity, begins to look attractive. But only to them. Most of us are too wedded to *ta blepomena*, the "things that are seen." The unbeliever scoffs at the notion of a life of blessedness, saying it is the product in imagination of a wretched life here like Paul's "afflictions." He thought he had a better warrant for belief than his present pain. It was the promise of a resurrected life, the certainty of faith that the one who raised the Lord Jesus would raise us up with him (v. 14). Paul wrote that he foresaw having to exchange one "tent" for another. He was in no more hurry to go than the rest of us but he firmly believed that taking up his new location was a reality the future would bring. We need to ask ourselves periodically whether we really believe in the promise.

GOSPEL: MARK 3:20-35

Last Sunday's Gospel passage (Mark 2:23-28[—3:6]) made the point that, for Jesus, like any good interpreter of the law, the relief of human need or service to others in distress came before religious observance. In today's lesson, 3:20-35, Jesus' family (v. 21), his mother and his brothers and sisters (v. 32), are reported as thinking him deranged. This tradition on the early anxiety of his kinsfolk is at odds with the scene John portrays at Cana of mother, brothers, and disciples in harmonious association (John 2:12) and later of Jesus' male relatives portrayed by Eusebius as a kind of Caliphate in the Jerusalem church. But here their dismay is genuine. Is he really "beside himself" (*exestē*, v. 21)? Possession by Beelzebub is the explanation provided by Mark's learned visitors from Jerusalem, probably the popular assumption that some "master of the house" has taken over (see Matt. 10:25)—like our modern "bats in the belfry." If *zebul*, "house," is intended and not *zibūl*, "dung," the dwelling in question is the heavenly residence of the pagan gods whom the Jews thought to be demons. The next attribution of Jesus' power—"by the ruler of the demons he casts out demons"—confirms the supposition. Such is not a very logical explanation of Jesus' supposed powers but logic never troubles antagonists whose minds are made up. Jesus counters their irrational explanation with logic, a logic of his own.

President Lincoln helped fix the Gospel phrase forever in the American mind with his "house divided" speech. Satan casting out Satan is as impossible an image as a nation continuing half-slave and half-free. This is as true today as when Jesus uttered it in the late 20s C.E. or Lincoln at the 1858 convention. Good and evil cannot coexist. Our technological culture has coined the term "to self-destruct." Jesus says of self-destruction in the demonic realm, "Never happened!" Evil protects evil, it does nothing to terminate it. Kingdoms and families torn by an evil principle, namely a murderous inner dissension, cannot survive (vv. 24-25).

Jesus proposes a second example, the thieves who must restrain a householder before they can get the job done (v. 27). Next, with a solemn declaration of assurance ("Truly I tell you," elsewhere unknown as an introductory phrase), Jesus enunciates the basic principle of opposition between good and evil. To attribute works of goodness to the evil one is the height of perversity. Speaking against the Son of man is allowable, in the Q form of this saying (Matt. 12:31-32 = Luke 12:10), but against the Holy Spirit never, as in Mark. The unforgivable, eternal sin against the Spirit that provides the exception to "all their sinful acts and blasphemies" that will be forgiven seems to be, from the context of vv. 22-30, obdurately refusing the forgiveness held out. The Holy Spirit's work is seen here as reconciliation. Only those who will not be reconciled cannot be reconciled.

In a concluding *logion* that brackets the opening phrase of the pericope (vv. 34-35; see v. 21), those who do God's will are declared kin to Jesus.

FIRST LESSON: GENESIS 3:1-21

The First Testament reading (Gen. 3:9-15, expanded before and after in EL) goes on the assumption introduced to the West by St. Augustine, following Wis. 2:24, that the serpent of Genesis 3 is Satan. Augustine was doubtless influenced by the declaration in John 8:44 that the devil was a murderer and a liar "from the beginning." Rabbinic interpretation knows nothing of this identification. A snake is a snake and, if poisonous, humanity's natural enemy. Any other understanding Jewish scholars consider unwarranted allegory. Their support comes from the punishment meted out to the serpent to go on its belly, in a sequence of etiologies that includes accounting for the pains of childbirth, the resistance of the soil, and the necessity of hard labor. These chapters account for almost everything except why the robin's breast is red (see Gen. 4:20-22). But the story of this reading is a tale about the origins of disobedience to God and must be taken seriously as such. Almost every people's saga of origins accounts for primordial wrongdoing and its consequences. The biblical tale is among the best.

Homilists would do ill to make anything special (as male expositors have done with tragic effect over the centuries) over the man-woman-snake sequence in the assignment of blame. It is a case of the universal rule of three in storytelling—an Englishman, a Scot, and an Irishman, or the mother bear, the father bear, and the little baby bear. Little is to be made of who told whom to do what. Neither is any time to be lost on snakes as eaters of dust (3:14). Let biblical literalists worry about that. All that is being said is that snakes and humans are fated to be natural enemies, "he" (the woman's seed or offspring, a masculine noun) clouting these reptiles on the head over the centuries and they biting human legs if they get the chance.

A few homilists at ease in patristic writings will know the typology of Mary as the crusher of the snake's head, influenced by the woman's victory over the dragon/serpent in Rev. 12:15-17. Christians familiar with statues of the Blessed Mother as having been conceived without sin (in archaic speech, "immaculate"), will recognize the rendering of the snake beneath her heel, often having a fruit in its distended jaws.

This is not a Sunday to discourse at length on natural history in Genesis or popular understandings in Semitic antiquity. It may be a day to speak about the evil we call sin. The concept and even the word may be in semiretirement but the reality is flourishing. Sin is not flaw or fault, it is moral evil. It is deliberate choice against human good, sometimes one's own but usually another's or just as often others'. Public life seems unacquainted with the idea of sin: "I seem to have made a wrong choice"; "It was a mistake"; "I confess to a bad error in judgment." All of these are cognitional stumblings. None is volitional. The sinner says: "I first craved, then took what was not mine to take: another's spouse, the public's money, the innocence of the young woman (or man) to whom I declared my love. It was a wicked thing to do. I beg God's forgiveness. I know that it cannot be forthcoming from a just God until I make recompense, insofar as that is possible, to the persons I wronged."

We call this a confession of sins. The easily spoken formulas of sorrow within public worship services may bear little relation to it. True confession knows what evil is. It recognizes the evil that was done and expresses heartfelt contrition for it and a firm purpose of amendment on that score. The opposite state of heart and mind the Gospel calls "eternal sin," a blasphemy against the Holy Spirit. This mentality denies that any grave injustice was done or else, acknowledging the fact, refuses to make amends. The old catechisms used to call this obduracy "impugning the known truth." A nation of churchgoers, we seem to be swimming in this evil.

ALTERNATIVE FIRST LESSON: 1 SAMUEL 8:4-20

The CL no longer proceeds to the account of Saul's melancholia that ended in violence toward David, as it did in the 1983 version (1 Sam. 16:14-23), but goes instead to the earlier explanation of how the monarchy came into existence (1 Sam. 8:4-20). Saul's enthronement is anticlimactic and adds nothing to the story (11:14-15). But the insight into the tendency of absolute power to corrupt absolutely is priceless. It means much in a democratic republic that has drifted toward an imperial presidency.

Fourth Sunday after Pentecost

Lutheran	Roman Catholic	Episcopal	Common Lectionary
Ezek. 17:22-24	Ezek. 17:22-24	Ezek. 31:1-6, 10-14	1 Sam. 15:34—16:13 or Ezek. 17:22-24
2 Cor. 5:1-10	2 Cor. 5:6-10	2 Cor. 5:1-10	2 Cor. 5:6-10, (11-13), 14-17
Mark 4:26-34	Mark 4:26-34	Mark 4:26-34	Mark 4:26-34

FIRST LESSON: EZEKIEL 17:22-24

Ezekiel 17:22-24 is the choice of the LL and RL while the EL looks elsewhere in the same book for a foreshadowing of Jesus' two seed parables of Mark 4:26-34. Before turning to the prophetic book we should simply note the first choice of the CL. The LORD is twice described as regretting having chosen Saul as king (1 Sam. 15:11, 35; cf. Gen. 6:6) because of his failure to exercise the ban (*herem*) on the Amalekites. Saul spared their king and much of their spoil for his own enrichment, not unlike the practices of third world monarchs and first world officeholders. The LORD then sends the priest Samuel to seek out David and anoint him secretly while Saul lives. There is a powerful lesson in the reminder, as the older sibling Eliab is rejected, that people see appearances but the LORD looks into the heart (16:7). It is muted somewhat when David's handsome appearance is praised (16:12; the work of another editor?)

Any homilist who hopes to be at ease in Ezek. 17:22-24, aside from seeing in the newly planted cedar shoot the model for Jesus' parable of the mustard bush (v. 23 = Mark 4:32), must at least read chap. 17 carefully from the beginning. The explanation of the nature fable in vv. 3-10 begins at v. 11, for which a rudimentary knowledge of events in Judah leading up to 600 B.C.E. is required. The king of Babylon is Nebuchadrezzar who, in 597 B.C.E., removed King Jehoiachin and took him and his princes into exile (17:12; cf. Jer. 22:24). He set his uncle, the twenty-one-year-old Zedekiah, son of King Jehoiakim, in his place (vv. 13-14). But Zedekiah rebelled toward the end of his tenth year on the throne, urged on by the Pharaoh Hophra (vv. 15-18; see 2 Kings 24–25). The great eagle who tore the top-most branch of the cedar and carried it off was Nebuchadrezzar (vv. 3-4). The other great eagle was Psammetichus II of Egypt with whom Zedekiah had made a treaty in 588. The east wind that would strike the transplanted noble vine, Judah (v. 10b), is the wrath of the LORD against Zedekiah for breaking the covenant treaty he had made with Nebuchadrezzar, calling on God as a witness (vv. 14-15).

This review should provide homilists and readers with the minimum knowledge for informing worshipers how to hear the allegory of Ezek. 17:22-24. Without some background it is almost purposeless to proclaim it publicly. Today's pericope does not occur in Ezekiel to prepare for Jesus' parable but there *is* a relation. Echoing the fable of vv. 1-10, this explanation sees in a future Davidic king a new sprig plucked from the lofty top of a cedar (see the "dynastic oracle" of 2 Sam. 7:13). The mountain height of Israel is Zion in Jerusalem, the birds in the new tree's branches are a sign of Judah's greatness to be (as of Assyria's, in the powerful lesson directed against the Pharaoh in 31:2-9). "If the cedar is the king of Judah, then the trees [of 17:24] are the kings of the surrounding nations" (Lawrence Boadt, *The New Jerome Bible Commentary*, 20:49 [Englewood Cliffs, N.J.: Prentice Hall, 1990], 318). This is a fable of the LORD's power both to bring high and to bring low. Without divine power and human trust in it, nothing is achieved.

GOSPEL: MARK 4:26-34

The first of Jesus' two parables in today's Gospel reading (Mark 4:26-34) is distinguished by being the only section in Mark without a parallel in Matthew or Luke. The two may have been coupled with the seed parable and its interpretation (4:3-20) before Mark's time in a "kingdom collection." The farmer, not the seed, is central to the first short story. His activity of sowing and his sleeping, ignorant of how nature does its work, then his harvesting, are the storyteller's main concern. The seed and how it sprouts and grows are matters of secondary interest. This parable (formally a similitude because the story is scarcely developed) and the one of the mustard seed that follows show, in the setting of the chapter, how central Jesus' kingdom message was for Mark's Gospel. The sowing process seems random ("scatter" being simply "cast" or "throw" in Greek). The farmer's control of it is nil until the grain has grown and it is time to put the sickle in (see Joel 3:13, Masoretic Text 4:13). The mystery of germination and growth is hidden from the farmer and so the parable is often designated that of "the seed growing silently." It might just as well be termed "the earth producing a crop" (v. 28) or "the mystified farmer" (v. 27c), so interrelated are the activities (and in his case the inactivities) of sower and seed.

Is the sower meant to be Jesus and the seed the word of the kingdom? Probably not, any more than the farmer is intended as a figure of God (despite the possible reference to the end time activity of God as harvester in Joel, found in v. 29) or of an early Christian evangelist. The silent growth of the seed and the harvest identify the parable as a defense of the kingdom's progress without the expected fanfare or violence. This progress is inevitable and it is a work of God. Human activity is essential but distinctly secondary.

Early in my teaching career a nursing student who was a major in the U.S. Army, a native of Owensboro, Kentucky, disputed the Gospel's statement that the mustard seed was "the smallest of all the seeds on earth" (4:31). She brought in tobacco and mustard seeds to prove it. The mustard seed couldn't cut it. It has taken tobacco forty years to diminish in influence in our culture relative to its size, but its seed is indeed tiny. Jesus was no agriculturalist, he was a worker in wood. The seed of the mustard plant suited his purpose well enough to illustrate diminutive size. It grows only to bushlike proportions, nothing like the majestic cedar of Ezekiel. But it does serve as a nesting-place for birds and that is all that the figure required.

The reign of God is under illustration here, a lively image in postbiblical Judaism that Jesus placed at the heart of his teaching. It survives in Judaism and the church as a figure of the willing submission of all creation to its LORD in time to come. For Christians the way to the kingdom is the church, but the church is not the kingdom. In Jesus' day many identified the reign of God as Israel's triumphant emergence over its pagan neighbors. Jesus made no such claim but described it rather as a work of God in human hearts that no earthly power could withstand.

The story is told, almost certainly apocryphal, of Napoleon's saying to Pope Pius VII whom he held captive for five years: "I will destroy that church of yours." That wise old man who was of the nobility before becoming a Benedictine monk said: "I doubt it. We priests have been trying to do it for eighteen centuries and have not succeeded." With all our follies we Christians, who are the church, have tried our best to humiliate it, betray its character, bring it low in the world's eyes. We have not succeeded because Jesus is the church's Lord and the Holy Spirit is its inner principle of life. Like the kingdom it leads to, the church is indestructible. On all the continents and remotest islands it "puts forth large branches, so that the birds of the air can make nests in its shade."

SECOND LESSON: 2 CORINTHIANS 5:1-17

The Pauline portion for today moves on to the next chapter from 2 Corinthians, 5:1-10 in LL and EL, with a slightly shorter reading in RL and a longer one in CL. The scandal of our inability to have a common Christian lectionary for the country is illustrated almost weekly. Committees are convinced they can do better—and of course they can. A parable of church disunity lies here. *Le mieux est l'ennemi du bien*, the French say—"The better is the enemy of the good." It is true. Our "better" has defeated our "good" over all the centuries in our disagreements over nonessentials. It is one thing for the churches to be divided over principle. It is quite another to be divided as a result of noncommunication, as in the case of the variant lectionaries.

Last week's reading concluded with 5:1 for the RL and CL. It begins with that verse today for the Lutheran and Episcopal churches. The difference between Paul's image of a risen life in 1 Corinthians 15 and the present passage have often been noted. There, the physical body is sown to be raised up a spiritual body (1 Cor. 15:44). Here Paul imagines a succession of dwellings (houses, tents). The earthly is destroyed, the heavenly is on file bearing our names, so to say, ready to clothe us (2 Cor. 5:1-2). Paul gets a little mixed in his metaphors when he tries to account for a slip-up in arrangements by speaking of the tragedy of nakedness overtaking us once the mortal coil has been shuffled off (v. 3). He speaks of an eagerness to be quit of the present burden of the body and a longing to be clothed anew—again, mildly fearful that the transition to phase two will not be smooth. He is rescued from his cloakroom confusion by the conviction that life will swallow up death. This is a certainty on which he knows we already have a guarantee, the Spirit. Mention of this personal pledge or first installment has already occurred in 1:22 and will be picked up again by the author of Ephesians at 1:14. In those other two places it is a double image. God puts a seal (*sphragis*) on us in giving the promised Holy Spirit, marking us as the Spirit's own. This creates confidence in believers like Paul who, even though they are "away from the Lord" while still in the body and prefer it otherwise, can see through faith what their eyes cannot see. Since judgment is sure with Christ as the judge on the basis of one's performance while living, the only thing to do is live so as to please him. And wait to be summoned.

Doris Day was almost an icon in her thirty years of filmmaking, recording, and television acting. The "girl next door" was the handsome older woman we might have expected in a recent television retrospective of her career. Musing unexpectedly on the traumas she has experienced in life, she wonders aloud if there is a heaven. In almost the same breath she concludes that her Carmel Valley home, close by her son and daughter-in-law, grandson, and her pets, is probably it.

But the Christian heaven has never been a painfree existence or an ideal piece of real estate. It has always meant being with Christ in his risen state and ours. St. Paul's attempts to imagine it are fumbling if well-intended tries. None of us can imagine that risen state. Paul does it best when he says that even now "everything is new." We walk by faith with respect to a life we cannot imagine. If we have had no experience in life of the Spirit who dwells in the church and in each of us ("living for [Christ]," 2 Cor. 5:15), we probably will not know how to behave once there. At least we will require some kind of remedial education.

Fifth Sunday after Pentecost

Lutheran	Roman Catholic	Episcopal	Common Lectionary
Job 38:1-11	Job 38:1, 8-11	Job 38:1-11, 16-18	1 Sam. 17: (1a, 4-11, 19-23), 32-49 *or* 1 Sam. 17:57—18:5, 10-16
2 Cor. 5:14-21	2 Cor. 5:14-17	2 Cor. 5:14-21	2 Cor. 6:1-13
Mark 4:35-41	Mark 4:35-41	Mark 4:35-41; (5:1-20)	Mark 4:35-41

GOSPEL: MARK 4:35-41 (5:1-20)

Jesus' teaching in parables beside the sea (Mark 4:1-33) concludes with the evangelist's observation that Jesus did not speak the word to "them"—presumably the crowds—except in parables, while explaining everything in private to his disciples (see v. 34). Mark makes Jesus' storytelling a technique for "those outside" (v. 11)—whom the Teacher, in any case, does not look upon as comprehending. He portrays Jesus' disciples as not faring much better in their grasp of the explanations offered. For Mark these potential insiders are little better off than the outsiders, in what is probably a warning to his contemporaries complacent in their belief.

All the lectionaries have as their Gospel pericope the end of the chapter that has contained five figurative expressions of God's impending rule (4:35-41). This passage goes with the next chapter (5:1-43) by sense, the first of four miracle accounts. This one manifests Jesus' power over nature. The others will show him victorious over Satan, sickness, and death. It is a miracle story in which Jesus' rebuke to the winds (v. 39) resembles what he might have said in exorcising demons. Paul Achtemeier coupled 4:35—5:43 with 6:34-44 as the first of two pre-Markan "catenae" or chains of miracle stories (*Journal of Biblical Literature* 89 [1970]: 265–91). He saw the second as 6:45-56; 8:22-26; and 7:24—8:10. Other exegetes divide the miracle accounts into collections of different lengths, while a few think that Mark found today's story already combined not only with 5:1-43 but also with the parables that go before it.

All such theories see the evangelist as a compiler rather than an author. If editing is his chief contribution, he is extremely clever at it, for his performance must be reckoned as far superior to that of the conveyers of fragments of tradition who preceded him.

Mark appears to have used Jesus' instructions to have a boat ready for him so that he would not be crushed by the crowd (3:7, 9-10) both as the introduction to his teaching in parables (4:1-34) and with a view to the present pericope (vv. 35-41). Most of the Markan miracle stories feature a plea for help or deliverance. Not so this one in which his companions lodge an accusation against the sleeping Jesus (v. 38c). His help follows and only after that a response. First, the storm is stilled. Only then does Jesus address his companions, this time with a charge of cowardice and lack of faith. Their being "filled with great awe" (v. 41a) masks in translation the cognate accusative that has them "fearing a great fear," a sure sign of the narrative's Semitic origins. Their response is not one of self-defense but of total consternation at the marvel they have just witnessed.

Mark's purpose in the telling then becomes clear. He wishes to underscore Jesus' power over wind and wave. At the level of literary construction, however, Achtemeier has noted that in the two cycles of miracle stories that he discerns, this one like the second is introduced by Jesus' calming of the sea. (See 4:39, preparatory to the miracles of chaps. 5 and 6, and 6:51, which introduces the miracle-chain of the end of chap. 6, then chaps. 7 and 8.) By placing Jesus' teaching in parables (4:1-33) between the exorcisms and healings of the first three chapters and the cures and nature miracles of the four chapters that follow it, the evangelist paints a picture of Jesus as authoritative in word and work. Jesus the Teacher is not a soft or gentle figure in Mark's Gospel. He is stern, peremptory, and powerful, the *pantokratōr* ("almighty one") of apsidal mosaics who looks upon those who claim belief in him with piercing, coal-black eyes.

FIRST LESSON: JOB 38:1-11, 16-18

Years ago I had a job in close association with a father and son, both born in Italy. The lad was eighteen or so but was still capable of immature behavior—pouting or sulking for the most part. Pietro would grow impatient with the boy Carlo and say to him angrily,

"Act as a man!" The father may not have mastered idiomatic English usage but he had his parental authority straight. The LORD rebukes Job in somewhat the same fashion in today's predominant first reading from the book of that name at 38:1-11. "Gird up your loins like a man," the voice comes out of the whirlwind (v. 3); in the REB translation, "Brace yourself and stand up like a man." The reasons for choosing the passage to foreshadow the stilling of the storm are evident. Not only does Israel's God begin the "YHWH speeches" of rebuke after the three troublesome comforters and Elihu finish chiding Job at great length, but does so in four unrelenting chapters that catalogue powers that are uniquely divine.

The storm passages are the special reason for the lectionary choice: "Who shut in the sea with doors when it burst out from the womb . . . prescribed bounds for it, and set bars and doors?" (vv. 8, 10). The obvious implication of the Gospel pericope is that Jesus did the same. The author of Job may have been as unsure of his cosmogony as Pietro was of his "like" and "as" but the effect is unmistakable. Puny Job, like the disciples in the boat, had best be careful of whom he charges with fault. King Canute of England in legend stood on the shore and commanded the proud waves: "Thus far and no farther!" They were as heedless of the royal command as the LORD hints the God of power will be of Job's complaints. In effect the challenger of God's justice is told, "Measure out the earth as you prepare to fashion it, while the stars look on. Deal with the raging sea like a babe in its crib whose soft clothing is the clouds and the darkness. Then come back to see me and we can talk." Job is put down by the sheer weight of God's glory, a word that in Hebrew means *weight*.

The Episcopal Lectionary adds vv. 16-18 of chap. 38 to the reading. It is a wise addition because in these verses the LORD asks Job directly whether he has accomplished any of these marvels in the cosmos, and challenges him: "Declare, if you know all this" (v. 18b). God does not so much act the bully as bring to the suffering Job's attention the infinite gap between divine wisdom, not simply divine power, and human weakness. What Job cannot comprehend is the design that underlies his fate. It is similar with the disciples. Their fear of drowning was perfectly natural but Mark is not telling a story that was in any sense natural. He is inculcating trust of a superhuman sort in God and God's Anointed. Fear is not the hallmark of Christian life. Faith is a matter of perfect trust.

ALTERNATIVE FIRST LESSON: 1 SAMUEL 17–18

The Common Lectionary reading from 1 Samuel 17–18, as customarily proposed for nonfestal seasons, does not prepare for hearing the Gospel. It simply continues the David story. While it recounts the bloody dispatching of Goliath, the Philistine champion (17:23), it is told for an edifying purpose, namely to show that the power of God is greater than the force of arms (17:45). The alternative reading is less violent, at least overtly, as it describes the seeds of Saul's psychotic envy.

SECOND LESSON: 2 CORINTHIANS 5:14—6:2

The semicontinuous reading from 2 Corinthians resumes from 5:14-21 of last week in the Lutheran and Episcopal lectionaries, stopping at v. 17 in RL but not until 6:2 in CL. The readings from this epistle on the two previous Sundays have Paul hinting that he is "wasting away," calling it a "slight momentary affliction" (4:16, 17; "the affliction we received in Asia," "the sentence of death," 1:8, 9?). He says, however, that his aim is to continue to please God whether in the body or "at home with the Lord" (5:9, 8). Paul hopes to conduct himself in such a way as to provide the Corinthians an opportunity to boast about him (v. 12). Outward appearance is not the norm as he expresses this hope. He banks on being well known to God and hopes the same can be said of them, whether "we are beside ourselves . . . or in our right mind" (v. 13). This phrasing may suggest temporary dementia as part of his affliction in Asia, whether from religious ecstasy, high fever, or some more deep-seated cause.

None of these troubles or the tensions existing between him and the community over one who has caused pain to both (see 1:23; 2:1-11) will keep him from preaching a doctrine of reconciliation in Christ. Love of him, the Christ who died and rose for all, is what urges Paul on in his mission. Nor did Christ die alone. In the corporate thinking of the apostle all died in him (5:14c). This means that all must live for him. The death all died was death to sin, the life is the new life of the baptized (see Rom. 6:10). The exact phrasing of 5:15 on this call to live for Christ and not for self occurs in a eucharistic prayer employed by some of the churches that do lectionary preaching.

As a consequence of Paul's faith in the dying and rising Christ, he looks at the whole world differently. He can view no one now as he did before, not even Christ (v. 16). *Kata sarka*, literally "according to the flesh," here means "with ordinary human knowledge." The opinion of Bultmann, Schoeps, and others that Paul used the phrase to indicate that he had no interest in the Jesus of history cannot be sustained. Paul is declaring that either he has ceased to conceive the Messiah in his former way or that his previous, dismissive view of Jesus has been proved invalid. The resurrection has changed everything for him. All is seen in a new light by those who share the apostle's faith. The "new [act of] creation," of v. 17 is the work of God in inaugurating the final age which Paul, as an eschatological thinker, puts in parallel with the creation of the world.

Paul's favoring of the term "in Christ' is well known (he uses it 165 times in his letters, including "in the Lord" and "in him"). Once the dust of fears that it may have a "mystical" meaning have settled (close to paranoia in some circles), it becomes evident that the phrase signifies a vital union between Christ and the believer bordering on symbiosis (see Joseph A. Fitzmyer, *Paul and His Theology, A Brief Sketch* [Englewood Cliffs: Prentice Hall, 1987], 89–90; also reprinted in *New Jerome Biblical Commentary*, p. 1409).

God is the one who achieves a reconciliation with alienated humanity. It is done through Christ. The noun for this restoration of friendship is *katallagē* and the verb *katalassein*. It is equivalent to justification, a legal or forensic expression, and sanctification. Such is the ministry (*diakonia*, v. 18) or being sent on embassy (*presbeuomen*, v. 20) that has been entrusted to Paul. He must proclaim this message of reconciliation.

There have not been apostles since the earliest age of the church but the responsibility to declare that "God and man are reconciled," in the words of the old English Christmas carol, has been passed on to us. "Be reconciled to God" (v. 20b) is a challenge that was first thrown to us at our birth in hereditary sin. The waters of baptism, energized by the Holy Spirit and responded to in faith, achieved the reconciliation. St. Paul puts it in the form of an entreaty to those among his Corinthian believers he has not found faithful to their calling. God has acted on our behalf (*hyper hemōn,* v. 21) by making Christ [to be] sin (*hamartian epoiēsen*) who knew no sin. This is perhaps the starkest paradox in all Christian Scripture. The All-Holy, the one in no need of redemption, becomes not a sinner but sin itself. Such is the length to which a merciful Father goes to reconcile us to God and to each other. And we say that we have not sinned, that we do not see any need to be forgiven! We who are the church are a collection of people ready to cast the first stone, who then discover a slight impediment in our reach. The apostle Paul has laid a charge upon us to which we must make adequate response.

Only one response is fitting. It is a prayer that the grace of God not be given us in vain (6:1). Without repentance we perish. We first need to know what sin is before salvation can mean anything to us. Justified we may be in our religious rhetoric, but sinners we undoubtedly are with a talent for not acknowledging the grim reality.

It is a warm summer day, this Fifth Sunday after Pentecost. Vacation time. Business is slow. Kids are out of school. It is as good a time as any—Paul called it "acceptable [to God]" (6:2) as did Isaiah (49:8)—to receive the grace held out, to repent of the ugly habits that impair our living fully in Christ, to become the righteousness of God. It is the only fitting response in thankfulness to the one who became sin for us.

Sixth Sunday after Pentecost

Lutheran	Roman Catholic	Episcopal	Common Lectionary
Lam. 3:22-33	Wisdom 1:13-15; 2:23-24	Deut. 15:7-11	2 Sam. 1:1, 17-27 or Wisdom 1:13-15; 2:23-24
2 Cor. 8:1-9, 13-14	2 Cor. 8:7-9, 13-15	2 Cor. 8:1-9, 13-15	2 Cor. 8:7-15
Mark 5:21-24a, 35-43 or 5:24b-34	Mark 5:21-43 or 5:21-24, 35b-43	Mark 5:22-24, 35b-43	Mark 5:21-43

FIRST LESSON: LAMENTATIONS 3:22-33

An anonymous late sixth-century author wrote five poems of lament over the destruction of Jerusalem by the Babylonians. They have been appended to the book of Jeremiah in the Greek tradition and are known as the "threnody," from the LXX *threnoi.* In Hebrew they occur in the "Writings." The first four of the poems are now four chapters. They are written as acrostics in which the separate stanzas begin with the successive letters of the Hebrew alphabet. Today's verses from chap. 3 begin with *beth* (22-24), *teth* (25-27), *yodh* (28-30) and *caph* (31-33), the eighth to the eleventh letter of the twenty-two-consonant alphabet. In general, these poems express repentance for sin, grief over the humiliation Zion has undergone, and submission to a well-deserved punishment. At the same time there is great confidence expressed in God's fidelity and hope for the restoration of the people in their own land.

The first twenty verses of chap. 3 are a catalogue of charges against God for the effects of the divine wrath leveled at the poet, who speaks for Israel. They are a tapestry of anger and despair: wormwood and gall; flesh wasted, bones broken; God a bear, a lion, a bowman poised with murderous intent. Then, in v. 21, the sun comes out. The threnodist has hope as he recalls "the steadfast love of the LORD . . . the mercies that never come to an end; they are new every morning" (vv. 22-23a). It is good to wait quietly for the LORD's salvation, says the threnodist, to turn one's cheek to the smiter and be filled with insults (vv. 26, 30). Why? Because this God will not reject forever. The causer of grief will yet have compassion, not being one who willingly afflicts or brings grief (vv. 31-33). We have a theodicy here, a defense of the providential design as vigorous as the attack on it that preceded it. This is a long look taken at Judah's recent humiliations, the reasoned reflection that the one who permits afflictions ("not willingly") has done it for the people's correction. The Most High may be the author of good and bad but it is either a punishment for sins or a means to have the people return to the LORD (vv. 38-40). The poem then returns to its earlier resentment at God's anger which has led to "the destruction of my people, (v. 48). It ends with a plea to the LORD to avenge Judah's enemies, indeed in a curse (vv. 64-66).

Christian prayer shrinks from these cries of the heart and, because it does, betrays biblical religion by its selectivity. Today's first lectionary reading picks its way gingerly through a powerful prayer, determined to improve the occasion. The psychiatrists who deal daily with repressed anger have something to say about Christianity's role in this matter.

ALTERNATIVE FIRST LESSON: WISDOM 1:13-15; 2:23-24; 2 SAMUEL 1:1, 17-27; DEUTERONOMY 15:7-11

The reasons for the Lutheran and Episcopal desertion of RL's Wisdom reading (1:13-15; 2:23-24) are twofold and obvious: the sixteenth-century decision to follow St. Jerome's *Hebraica veritas* by not considering six books of the LXX canonical Scriptures; and, in the Episcopal tradition (adopted by the CL), which is not kept from proclaiming them publicly by this scruple, their absence from many pulpit Bibles. The Wisdom selection of RL (1:13-15; 2:23-24) presents the Hellenist Jewish view that God did not create death, but rather made humanity for incorruption in the divine image. It was "through the devil's envy death entered the world, and those who belong to his company experience it" (v. 24). The way this passage foreshadows the resuscitation of Jairus's daughter in the Gospel reading is clear.

The CL report of David's lament over the deaths of Saul and Jonathan follows last Sunday's reading about the killing of Goliath and Saul's growing envy of David. Today's song is one of triumph over Amalek but also a hymn of forgiveness.

The EL usually opts for a first reading that correlates with the second rather than the Gospel. "Give liberally and be ungrudging" (Deut. 15:10) is the LORD's response to the half-verse quoted in the gospel, "The poor you have always with you" (Deut. 15:11; cf. Mark 14:7).

SECOND LESSON: 2 CORINTHIANS 8:1-15

The Deuteronomy appeal to be generous to the poor and needy matches perfectly the exhortation of Paul in 2 Cor. 8:7, 9, 13-15 to respond with generosity to his collection for the famine-stricken Jewish believers of Jerusalem: "Though [Jesus Christ] was rich, yet for your sakes he became poor, so that by your poverty you might become rich" (v. 9). Paul wants to see a fair balance between the abundance of the one group and the need of the other (see 2 Cor. 8:13-14). In v. 15 he quotes Exod. 16:18 on the gathering of the manna where God miraculously equalized what each collected. Nothing was left over, neither was there any shortage. He wishes it to be the same between the well-fixed Corinthians and the starving Jerusalemites. The terms of St. Paul's appeal are ingenious. This eighth chapter and the ninth that follows it should be the subject of regular study for anyone who must regularly beg contributions, especially for those more needy than the contributors. The giving of the rich Christ who impoverished himself for our sakes is the first paradigm (v. 9). The abundance of the believers in Judea who had the Gospel first, relative to the latecomers to the gospel in Achaia, is the second (vv. 14-15). The touch of genius lies in v. 13, where the apostle claims to have no wish to pressure his Corinthians as they provide relief for others (after having outrageously put forward the good example of the Macedonians, vv. 1-5!). For Paul it is a simple matter of turnabout being fair play, however that might be said in Greek. Modern congregations are too seldom reminded of the wealth they have in the Gospel despite their possibly being straitened financially. Appeals for support can make sense to people if they are put on a theological basis of some depth, not just the timeworn "God will not be outdone in generosity" or even the Pauline "God loveth a cheerful giver" (2 Cor. 9:7). The omission of vv. 10-12 from the Lutheran Lectionary, incidentally, may save Paul from redundancy, but what preacher is not redundant when it comes to money?

GOSPEL: MARK 5:21-43

The Gospel pericope, which tells of two miracles of healing (Mark 5:21-43), follows the miraculous stilling of the storm of the previous Sunday (4:35-41). While it is true that Mark's Gospel is "a book of miracles," homilists must never lose sight of why he tells these tales. He is at pains to show Jesus as God's man who points to the final age that he inaugurates with deeds of power. Mark also has a distinct point to make in each story he tells, gleaned it would seem from a variety of sources. Thus, in today's passage, despite similarities in vocabulary ("faith," "fear," "well" or "sound," "daughter"), the grammatical style of the two narratives (5:21-24, 35-43, and 25-34) is sufficiently different to argue for two distinct origins. (Daniel J. Harrington in *The New Jerome Biblical Commentary*, 41:36, p. 607). Mark has made here one of his numerous intercalations, a story within a story—see 1:21-28; 2:1-12; 6:7-30; 11:12-21. This technique has led the Lutheran and Episcopal lectionaries to eliminate the middle narrative, vv. 35-43, possibly so that hearers and homilists will be spared confusion over the relation of the two.

Jesus and his disciples return to the west shore of the lake (v. 21), having gone across to the region between the east shore and Gerasa (4:35; 5:1). This seems to be part of the pattern of several crossings used by Mark to link up Jews and non-Jews as the objects of Jesus' concern. The petitioner in the first story, Jairus, a Jewish official, besides being a distraught father, is an example of the well-placed as well as the peasantry seeking aid from Jesus through trust in him (vv. 34, 28). The girl is "approaching the end" in Mark but already dead in Matthew and Luke, a heightening of the wonder. Jesus is asked to lay his hands on her to achieve the cure (v. 23). In the internal story the contact is reversed as the favored woman touches Jesus' cloak (vv. 28-29). Mark uses the girl's lifetime of twelve years (v. 42) as the length of the woman's suffering (v. 25) to link up the two accounts. The child's life seems to be over at the same length of time as the woman's ritually disqualifying issue of blood (Lev. 15:25-30). Jesus restores both to life and health, the woman instantaneously and without a ritual gesture, the girl after an interval and in a dramatic setting. *Talitha cum* is Aramaic (see also 3:17; 7:11, 34; 11:9, 10; 14:36; 15:22, 34). The injunction to silence is part of Mark's keeping Jesus' identity secret until 15:39. Jesus' declaration that she is only sleeping is not to be taken literally. It signals what he means to do. In both cases the verb translated "made well" or healed is *sōzein*, "save," while "live" and "life," prominent in the story of Jairus' daughter, will take on a theological meaning after Jesus' resurrection. This is, in fact, the meaning of these two interlaced stories. They are not simply wonders showing the power of God in Christ. They are illustrations of the restoration of dead souls in Mark's time and ours.

Seventh Sunday after Pentecost

Lutheran	Roman Catholic	Episcopal	Common Lectionary
Ezek. 2:1-5	Ezek. 2:2-5	Ezek. 2:1-7	2 Sam. 5:1-5, 9-10 or Ezek. 2:1-5
2 Cor. 12:7-10	2 Cor. 12:7-10	2 Cor. 12:2-10	2 Cor. 12:2-10
Mark 6:1-6	Mark 6:1-6	Mark 6:1-6	Mark 6:1-13

GOSPEL: MARK 6:1-13

There is relative unanimity among the lectionaries on this summer Sunday's readings, with only a little variation among the verses. In starting with the Gospel pericope, Mark 6:1-6, it may be well to recall to weekly worshipers the progress of readings from this Gospel since the feast of Pentecost. Beginning with the Second Sunday (= 9th *in anno* of RL; Proper 4 of CL), which employed Mark 2:23-28 on plucking grain on the Sabbath, the readings have been about Beelzebub and a house divided (3:20-35, Third Sunday), the earth producing of itself and the mustard seed (4:26-34, Fourth Sunday), the calming of the storm (4:35-41, Fifth Sunday), and the resuscitation of Jairus's daughter (5:21-24a, 35-43, Sixth Sunday). That latest deed of power was worked in the unnamed place where Jairus was a local leader. Mark now situates Jesus in his hometown. The selections up to this point have been: stories of conflict, two parabolic teachings, a nature miracle, and two miracles of return to life and health. There have been positive and negative responses to Jesus in this activity in Galilee. It will be capped by his rejection in Nazareth along with a group of unnumbered disciples (cf. Luke 4:16-30, which puts the incident at the beginning of Jesus' mission).

Synagogues here and elsewhere in the Gospels are places of all kinds of assembly, including teaching and prayer. Distinct buildings for the latter purposes seem to be a much later development. The astonishment at Jesus' deeds of power and wisdom (v. 2) is compounded by familiarity with him and his family. His trade or craft is known, as well as his family members. "Son of Mary" would have been unusual in the culture since parentage was reckoned by fathers.

Even if Joseph were dead it would not explain the usage and is perhaps intended as an insult. Catholics and Protestants have long divided themselves on doctrinal lines as to whether his four named *adelphoi* were siblings, ever since St. Jerome insisted that Mary was "ever virgin" *(aeiparthenos = semper virgo)*. The present writer does not think that the New Testament and Hellenist Jewish writings provide a definitive answer. If it did, Catholics and conservative evangelicals would have to accept Mary's motherhood of many children. Rudolf Pesch (1976) and John P. Meier (1991), however, both Catholics, argue that the minimum of six mentioned in Mark 6:3 were also born to Mary.

Some of the ambiguities attending both positions, among them those raised by Mark 15:40, 47; 16:1 about the motherhood of James and Joses, are discussed by R. Brown, K. Donfried, J. Fitzmyer, and J. Reumann, eds., in *Mary in the New Testament* (Philadelphia and New York: Fortress and Paulist, 1978), 65–72. Two are Lutherans, two are Catholics; they come into agreement that "it cannot be said that the NT identifies them *without doubt* as blood brothers and sisters and hence as children of Mary," and on three other points. But they do not agree on the most likely solution to the problem created by the three places in Mark cited above where James and Joses seem to be sons of another Mary.

The discussion here is intended to keep homilists from the diversion of taking a stand on something that cannot be known with certainty. It is clear that Jesus' family, however constituted, was well known locally and became part of the reason his townspeople "took offense at him" (v. 3). This elicited Jesus' proverbial saying that prophets are honored everywhere except in their homeplace and among their nearest kin (v. 4; par. Matt. 13:58; Luke 4:24; John 4:44). It is not likely that the remembered proverbial saying led to the story, since John's Gospel provides independent testimony that "not even his brothers believed in him" (7:5).

Mark means to conclude his section on the miracles and teaching in Galilee that were received variously with an account of Jesus' rejection in his own town. His non-acceptance there should not be interpreted more broadly than in that limited Galilean setting. Mark, it is true, is adding another building block to the earlier plotting of Pharisees and Herodians he has cited (3:6). We cannot reconstruct from the Gospels the exact alignment of the learned, the political, and simple folk for and against Jesus. Only the implacable enmity he aroused among the Temple priesthood and the skepticism of members of his family come through clearly. Mark has Jesus incapable of deeds of power in his hometown because of local unbelief but he immediately softens this judgment (v. 6b). Matthew eliminates any mention of incapacity (13:58) and Luke in 4:16-30 omits speaking of it altogether.

Homilists need to underscore the way Mark is constructing his narrative rather than conveying literal truth in the details he has from his sources. The evangelist is anxious above all, as any preacher or teacher should be, to frame powerful lessons for his contemporaries. He is concerned about complacency and any reasons people might have for dismissing Jesus and his message. Fear of losing position or power is first among these. The suspicion that Jesus is a quite ordinary, gifted Jewish teacher of his time is another. Popular reports of what scholars have concluded lately, "findings" that are themselves journalism marked by a heavy bias, proliferate in our day. Even those long familiar with Jesus from church and Sunday school attendance acquire reasons, often in the realm of personal morality, to dismiss him as a true prophet. People have been dividing themselves over him ever since Mark's day—and for roughly the same reasons now as then.

FIRST LESSON: EZEKIEL 2:2-5

All the lectionaries select Ezekiel 2:2-5 (the CL as an alternative only) as the passage they think best foreshadows the refusal of those in Jesus' hometown to honor him as a prophet. The problem with it is the same as with today's Gospel reading from Mark 6. Christian hearers of both are likely to engage in projection, attributing rebellion and stubbornness to Jews generally instead of to Ezekiel's sixth-century people of Judah in exile and Mark's hostile Galileans. When the Bible is read in Christian circumstances it must always be heard as addressed to Christian hearers. They no less than the ancients are presumed derelict in heeding God's word. The rebelliousness and impudence attributed to the people of the southern kingdom (vv. 3, 4) is even greater as regards Christians, in light of the further revelation they claim. Consequently, any homiletic treatment of the first reading in relation to the Gospel or the two taken together needs to beam the biblical strictures at modern hearers and not just ancient ones. This is part of the problem of not reading the Bible as an anti-Jewish book written by some other ethnic stock. Since Jews composed it, it can be considered the world's outstanding example of self-scrutiny by a people. When Christians read it they must see in the Bible a collection of tracts against themselves, since they claim continuity with the people Israel and have adopted these sacred books as their own.

The priest Ezekiel, son of Buzi (1:3), is the seer addressed by the speaker who is Israel's God. The contrast is highlighted by the use of the address "mortal" or "human one" (lit., "son of man"), used more than ninety times. He is invested with God's "spirit" as an intermediary and sent with a message to the recalcitrant people, thus described five times in three verses and then "scorpions" and "briars." The prophet is told not to fear their words or be dismayed by their looks but speak to them courageously. "They shall know" is a phrase that appears often in this book, a kind of signature that God has acted. All this leads up to the injunction to eat a scroll written on both sides which, though filled with lamentation and woe, proves sweet as honey upon an eating (2:9—3:3, cf. Jer. 15:16; Rev. 10:9-10). This figure for the joyful acceptance of the word of God gives special meaning to the Book of Common Prayer's "read, mark, and inwardly digest."

It has been correctly observed that the prophecies of Ezekiel are dire for the most part but with chap. 37 they turn consolatory and remain such through 40–48. Today's reading is from the earlier, grimmer section.

ALTERNATIVE FIRST LESSON: 2 SAMUEL 5:1-5, 9-10

The Common Lectionary reading for this Sunday (which it designates Proper 9) is 2 Samuel 5:1-5, 9-10. David has been anointed king by the people of Judah, his own tribe, at Hebron (2 Sam. 2:4). Now all the tribes of north and south assemble there for what is described as a second anointing. The "covenant" with the elders of

Israel (v. 5) was probably a capitulation as David went from strength to strength (vv. 9-10).

SECOND LESSON: 2 CORINTHIANS 12:2-10

To begin 2 Corinthians 12 at v. 7b as the Lutheran and Roman lectionaries do gives a strange impression of what is going on in this part of the letter. The first six and one-half verses of the chapter speak with satisfaction and gratitude (Paul uses the word "boast") of the visions and revelations he has received. He speaks periphrastically of "a person" to whom all this has happened. Then, in an abrupt switch, he describes a thorn in the flesh (*skolops tē sarki*, v. 7), a satanic messenger that has accompanied the gifts to keep him from too great elation. Everything conceivable, both physical and psychological, hinted at in Paul's other letters, has been proposed as this thorn including enemies among his own associates. It is impossible to know what he has in mind. He reports that his prayers to be delivered from the torment have been unavailing. They have elicited, however, a divine response that has become a treasured watchword of Christians: "My grace is sufficient for you, for power is made perfect in weakness" (v. 9a). The first phrase has entered into Western theological discourse as a kind of battle cry in wars over merely sufficient grace and what God has foreordained to give as the help against temptation. That is not Paul's concern. He launches into a paean to his weaknesses, for without them God's power would have no opportunity to work in him. What others might regret as shortcomings and setbacks Paul does not. These "weaknesses" in the eyes of others he revels in (v. 10).

The words of certain teachers echo more strongly from one's past, it seems, than any word from a classic, even a scriptural source. A college instructor in Latin who was a formidable grammarian can still be heard in the mind's ear fulminating against those for whom the sequence of tenses or the subjunctive mood in clauses of purpose or result was a *terra incognita*: "Regret their ignorance, gentlemen? Not in the least. They *glory* in their infirmities!" To such purpose was 2 Corinthians 12:9 put in this writer's youth. It has helped remind him over the years that weaknesses divinely imposed may be exulted in but the self-induced through laziness or careless omission, never.

Eighth Sunday after Pentecost

Lutheran	Roman Catholic	Episcopal	Common Lectionary
Amos 7:10-15	Amos 7:12-15	Amos 7:7-15	2 Sam. 6:1-5; 12b-19 or Amos 7:7-15
Eph. 1:3-14	Eph. 1:3-14 or 1:3-10	Eph. 1:1-14	Eph. 1:3-14
Mark 6:7-13	Mark 6:7-13	Mark 6:7-13	Mark 6:14-29

SECOND LESSON: EPHESIANS 1:1-14

The lectionaries begin a new epistle today, Ephesians. The longest span of the reading chosen by all is 1:1-14. The salutation of vv. 1-2 is probably omitted by the Lutheran and Roman lectionaries because "in Ephesus" does not occur in the first verse of the earliest and best manuscripts but also because of its doubtful character as a genuine letter. It is more a treatise directed to the newly baptized, like 1 Peter. Moreover, the phrases, "I have heard of your faith . . . and your love" (1:15), and "surely you have already heard of the commission . . . that was given me for you" (3:2) cannot have been written by Paul, whom Acts 19:10 speaks of as having resided at Ephesus for two years. What we seem to have here is a faithful anthology of Paul's thought arranged for circulation among those who have not known him and given the character of a personal letter (see 1:15-23; 3:1-13; 4:1; and 6:21-23, the first two verses of which duplicate Col. 4:7-8). Besides the last duplication cited there are numerous other indications that the compiler of Ephesians knew Colossians, although he uses some words and phrases with a different meaning. Whatever the circumstances of its authorship, it is a remarkable piece of writing that has given the church some of the most memorable Pauline phrases.

The blessedness of God that has resulted in a blessing in Christ is hymned throughout vv. 3-14. This passage is punctuated three times by "for the praise of [God's] glory" (vv. 6, 12, and 14). Editors of the Greek text create new sentences at vv. 7, 11, and 13 but in fact they are probably relative clauses beginning "in whom" rather than "in him." All twelve verses are a single sentence, a feat made possible by clauses such as the above and prepositions, word plays, parallellisms, and chains of synonyms like "will . . . purpose . . . plan." The word "forgiveness" (*aphesis*) of v. 7 is not used by Paul and occurs only here and in Col. 1:14 in the Pauline corpus. It is, however, a favorite of Luke's as part of the phrase, "the forgiveness of sins." Paul seems to be quoting a formula already in place when he speaks in Rom. 3:25 of God's "passing over (*paresis*) of sins previously committed," from which the Ephesians word could be derived.

The phrase "in the heavenly places" of v. 3 is peculiar to this epistle, being found also at 1:20; 2:6; 3:10; 6:12. In the first three instances the reference is benign, as it describes the presumed dwelling place of God and the glorified Christ, who is far above "all rule and authority and power and dominion" (1:21). In 3:10 it could be neutral: The mysterious plan of God is "made known to the rulers and authorities in the heavenly places"; but these spirits are clearly malignant in 6:12: "the cosmic powers of this present darkness . . . the spiritual forces of evil in the heavenly places." "Heavenly places" (*epouraniois*) in all cases must be the heavens in general where God and Christ and the baleful spirits, in the cosmology of that time, were all thought to reside.

These conceptions of another age are not relevant to the people of our age. Important to us is the stress on the divine election (vv. 4, 5, 11) that has bestowed on us grace in profusion, redemptive through Christ's blood; forgiveness of trespasses; an inheritance, the Gospel of salvation and the seal of the promised Holy Spirit, a pledge toward the redemption of a people (vv. 6, 7, 11, 13, 14). All Christians believe in the predestination of those who will end in God's presence. It is the predestination of the reprobate, if there be any such, over which they are divided. But the lengthy blessing that is today's second reading says nothing of this. It is all praise of the divine plan to redeem us, hidden in the innermost reaches of godhead for long ages as mystery but now revealed. Ephesians starts out, not by declaring, "Go, tell it on the mountain," but "Go tell it in the heights of heaven that God's own people has been delivered from servitude to the powers." Such is the way the mystery of human redemption is couched in terms understandable to a church of former pagans, not Jews, that would prove to be the church of the future.

FIRST LESSON: AMOS 7:7-15

Amos's utter honesty before the hostile priest of the shrine at Bethel, Amaziah, is doubtless thought to foreshadow the reception met with by Jesus' disciples sent out on mission. This herdsman and pruner of trees is a man of the south active at a northern sanctuary during the long reign of Jeroboam II of Israel (786–746 B.C.E.). The king's hired prophet tries to send Amos packing to his homeland but the man of Judah proclaims all the louder his prophetic call and message. Families shall be broken up, prophets and kings die, and Israel go into exile (Amos 7:17). Prosperity has tragically stopped up the ears of the northern king and his prophets alike. They will not hear of the Assyrian threat. The voice of complete candor has to be stilled. It is more than officialdom can bear.

ALTERNATIVE FIRST LESSON: 2 SAMUEL 6:1-5, 12b-19

In the CL pericope for this Sunday the ark of the covenant is brought in stages to the city of David. There the king dances before it and is despised by his wife Michal for doing it. He opts for the LORD in the face of her scorn.

GOSPEL: MARK 6:7-29

Jesus' message was like that of Amos, whether in delivering it himself or entrusting it to the twelve whom he sent out two by two (Mark 6:7). It seemed to work for them as it has for him. Just as in Jesus' early career, demons were expelled and many of the sick were cured. In describing the first sending of the disciples Mark employs the technique of intercalation encountered in chap. 5, the miracle within a miracle. In this case it begins with the disciples' instructions by Jesus on how to act in his name (6:6b-13) and ends with their return, reporting to him "all that they had done and taught" (v. 30). In between Mark places the account of the death of the Baptist. A usual feature of his "sandwich" technique, which is minimal in the daughter of Jairus and hemorrhaging woman narrative, is to be found here, that is, the light cast on the outer story by the inner one. John the Baptist's fate may well be that of the itinerant exorcists and preachers of repentance (vv. 7, 12). Discipleship of Jesus can involve the harassment visited on Amos, the imprisonment and death of the son of Zechariah. Today's pericope marks a turning point in the Markan Gospel. Jesus' rebuff in Nazareth causes him to turn elsewhere in Galilee and share his mission with his associates. The detailed instructions about their conduct on the road describe the detachment of itinerant philosophers and religious teachers.

Amaziah in the first reading is a familiar type of representative of religion, the courageous Amos another, and the dispropertied Jesus and his disciples still a third. Every Christian has a share in the roles of prophet, priest, and king proper to the Master. At baptism each person is constituted to some degree a spokesperson, an intermediary, and a bearer of rule. Circumstances differ but the elements common to all are the courage needed to exercise these roles and the necessity to "travel light" in order to disarm evil and get the message heard. Normal Christians fail on one front or the other. Intimidation results in compromise or silence. The challenge to live simply is answered by multiplied acquisition. Why should these things be? Why among a company where heroism should be the rule is it the exception?

A week-long silence about deepest-held convictions ensues after Sunday worship while the fanatical few embarrass the rest by proclaiming a twisted version of the Gospel's demands. Christian politicians pocket their principles to get elected and the people's money once they are elected. In their sex lives Christians will not let the church, that enemy of human freedom, dictate to them but mean to follow their consciences, which sternly dictate the most pleasure for the least penalty.

Amaziah always seems to hold the best cards while Amos cannot muster a pair of deuces. Some disciples cast out demons and anoint and cure, but the places that require the shaken dust of rejection are far more numerous than the receptive towns. Sir Edmund Burke thought he was enunciating a political principle when he spoke of the evil that follows when good people do nothing. He may have been talking about people who say they live by the gospel.

Ninth Sunday after Pentecost

Lutheran	Roman Catholic	Episcopal	Common Lectionary
Jer. 23:1-6	Jer. 23:1-6	Isa. 57:14b-21	2 Sam. 7:1-14a or Jer. 23:1-6
Eph. 2:13-22	Eph. 2:13-18	Eph. 2:11-22	Eph. 2:11-22
Mark 6:30-34	Mark 6:30-34	Mark 6:30-44	Mark 6:30-34, 53-56

GOSPEL: MARK 6:30-44, 53-56

The gripping account of the beheading of John the Baptist (Mark 6:14-29) has been omitted in the readings between last Sunday and this. It does not occur as a reading on any Sunday nor does the parallel, Matt. 14:3-12. The RL employs the Markan narrative as a weekday reading (Friday, fourth Week) and the churches that observe a feast of the beheading of John (August 29) read it as the Gospel of the day.

Today's pericope in the Lutheran and Catholic lectionaries (6:30-34) is not heavily laden with content. It takes up immediately where last Sunday's Gospel had left off at v. 13 with the "apostles" (6:30; the only use of the term in Mark, perhaps a contrast with John's "disciples" in v. 29), returning and reporting to Jesus all they have done and taught. The next verses tell of Jesus' invitation to them, so besieged and occupied are they, to come apart and rest awhile. They depart in a boat only to encounter the great crowd that has preceded them on foot along the lakeshore. Jesus in his compassion for them in their unshepherded condition (cf. Ezek. 34:5-6) begins to teach them. This brief passage is the second bracket that encloses the grisly tale of the Baptist's execution. (See last week's commentary for Mark's sandwich technique.) It also serves as an introduction to what follows, this evangelist's first account of the multiplication of the loaves. The Episcopal Lectionary provides that story (vv. 35-44). Five readings from John 6 will interrupt the Markan flow in all the lectionaries but the Episcopal, which gives only four. It turns to Mark 6:45-52, the walking on the sea, next Sunday. The others leave this narrative to the Matthew year (Lutheran, twelvth Sunday after Pentecost), the parallel to Mark that the Episcopal also employs.

FIRST LESSON: JEREMIAH 23:1-6

Ezekiel is not alone in citing the figure of sheep without a shepherd (34:5-6). Jeremiah does the same obliquely by referring to the people's shepherds as neglectful and dispersive of their flocks (23:1-6). The passages in the books of prophecy may derive from Num. 27:17 or 1 Kings 22:17. In any case, today's first reading is directly suggested by the Markan reference to the uninstructed crowds as sheep without a shepherd (6:34). The God of Israel of old promised woe to destructive shepherds (Jer. 23:1) and promised to respond by restoring the remnant to their own fold. Unquestionably the reference here is to a time in the future when the LORD will raise up a Davidic Branch (*tsemaḥ*, a shoot or scion, meaning here a descendant) who will reign wisely and justly (v. 5). A series of oracles against the successors of Josiah has preceded this pericope. They are Shallum (22:11, called by his throne name Jehoahaz in 2 Kgs. 23:31-32), Jehoiakim (Jer. 22:13-19; see 2 Kgs. 23:34), the latter's eighteen-year-old son Jehoiachin (vv. 20-30), also known by the abbreviated form Coniah. We might have expected an oracle against Zedekiah next, surely no favorite of Jeremiah, but the prophet contents himself with a reference to him in 23:6 by a pun on his name *Sidqiyahu*, which means "My justice is YHWH," calling the future king "YHWH *sidqenu*" meaning "Our God is our justice." In the days of that predicted one not only will Judah be in safety but also the northern kingdom Israel (v. 6).

Homilists need to remember that the neglected and willful shepherds of the prophets' fulminations were kings, not prophets or priests. Christian clergy derelict in their duty are under censure only in a transferred sense. Preachers have to be wary when they target publicly the shepherds of the Bible, namely civic and political leaders. Abuses of power that are well known and widespread need to be denounced publicly but the offenders are unwisely referred to by name. Threats of suit for slander quite apart, the courageous cleric can always say: "If the shoe fits, wear it. I named no one." Partisans of officeholders who are suspect of stealing public moneys, of torture, or murder can always decry politics in the pulpit but the common people are not deceived. They are the greatest sufferers and they welcome a ministerial or priestly voice. They know instinctively that ordained ministry brings with it the guardianship of both public and private morals. Any such outspokenness will be exercised at a high price. Jeremiah was carted off to Egypt (Jeremiah 43–44) where we lose all track of him but not before a few unpleasant incidents in a dungeon and a miry cistern. The proclaimer of the Gospel who spells out its implications will pay, one way or another.

Laying bare bad shepherding practice within the church is a delicate, not to say a dangerous business. It is always allowable to declare before the assembly one's own sins and shortcomings: "I have not visited the sick faithfully. I have neglected Christian education woefully. I regularly favor the moneyed class in this congregation." These are sermons we have not heard lately. It can be a disedifying matter to share with congregation members all that one has against the church officials to whom one is beholden. They do not know about preachers' peculiar pain and they are not helped by hearing about their resentments. Yet some dereliction of churchly duties do touch people's lives intimately and must be spoken of. Whole peoples have been lost to Christian unity by absentee or high-living clergy, by clerical struggles for power, by gross moral injustices on a local scene. These things must be preached about, at the proper time, in the proper way, after much thought and prayer. Passages like Jer. 23:1-6 are helpful here. The inspired word often says what human instruments could not say half so well.

The prophet Nathan tells David in the CL reading that he need not fret about not having built a house for the LORD. A house of another sort is in God's plan, a dynasty that will last forever (2 Sam. 7:11c-14a).

SECOND LESSON: EPHESIANS 2:11-22

With a comment on Eph. 2:11-22 our work will be finished. This writing of the Pauline school is especially valuable to the church. The church of then is so almost entirely gentile that St. Paul's discussions of the Mosaic law and his rabbinic illustrations can have little meaning for most of its members. "You Gentiles by birth" (v. 11; cf. 3:1) are being reminded by an anonymous, ethnically Jewish writer that their religious background was pretty thin gruel: They not only had no

Christ in their lives but no preparation for him. Without knowing of "the covenants of promise" they were, in Jewish eyes, without hope (v. 12). The old antipathy between the circumcised and uncircumcised was very much a part of their experience, both in youth and right up to the present. This is a matter of some importance for modern Christians. Having had no background of Jewishness, they are impoverished, disadvantaged, and they may not forget it. Gentile Christians have trouble understanding their own Scriptures, which would not be the case if they had a Semitic mentality and language.

At the time of Ephesians the churches of Asia Minor were still made up, however, of Jews and non-Jews, the "near" and the "far off" of Isa. 57:19 referred to in 2:13. The Pauline author sees the two previously irreconcilable groups brought into one by the blood of Christ who "is our peace" (v. 14). The "abolishing" of the law (*katargēsas* is the verb form and it means that) is a stronger term than one can imagine Paul using except in the sense of its ritual ordinances as applied to Gentiles. The coexistence of Jews and Gentiles in the one body of Christ was a reality of a century or so and even at that in small numbers. The old hostility, declared put to death by the cross (v. 16), was resurrected in the second century by a Gentile church. Tragically, challenges concerning responsibility for the cross became the occasion for reerecting the dividing wall.

The peace that should have marked relations between Jews and Gentiles ever since Jesus' day, whether the two made up one body in him or not, has not been realized. Each side opted to be divided over this Jew who was a man of peace. But faith in him cannot be shown to be the sole point at issue. Ethnicity and language played their part. So did differing interpretations of what it meant to be faithful to the tradition. Pride and passion, moreover, were absent from neither side.

Non-Jewish believers in Christ are those who are being addressed in Ephesians. They are the "we" of the church of the centuries. Our alien condition as members of the household of God has been over since we adopted the religion of Israel, the religion of Jesus, as our own. He is the stone at the corner of a living temple. It has one wall largely missing, the other disfigured by the gaps of apostasy and deep-seated hatreds. Yet it is "a holy temple in the Lord" in God's design, for those who have faith in Christ. We Gentile Christians may never forget that. We will, for all time, be something of the Jews through all the prophets of an older time and that Jew we call "our Lord."